THE INDIAN IN AMERICAN HISTORY

Children at the Crow Indian reservation school, Montana, about 1900. *(Montana Historical Society)*

THE INDIAN IN AMERICAN HISTORY

Edited by FRANCIS PAUL PRUCHA
Marquette University

HOLT, RINEHART AND WINSTON
New York • Chicago • San Francisco • Atlanta
Dallas • Montreal • Toronto • London • Sydney

Cover illustration: Portrai of a Jicarilla Apache from
New Mexico. *(American Museum of Natural History)*

CONTENTS

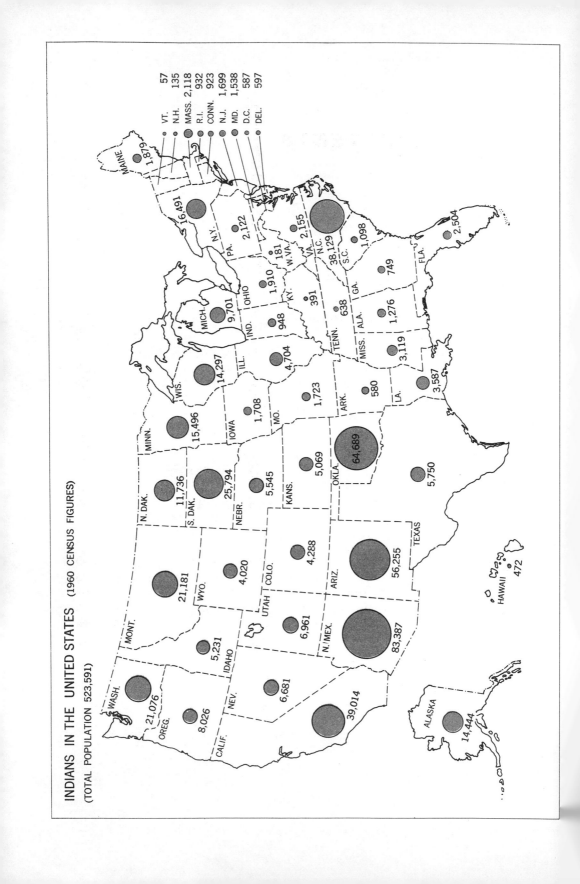

INDIANS IN THE UNITED STATES (1960 CENSUS FIGURES)
(TOTAL POPULATION 523,591)

VT.   57
N.H.   135
MASS. 2,118
R.I.   932
CONN.   923
N.J.   1,699
MD.   1,538
D.C.   587
DEL.   597

MAINE 1,879

N.Y. 16,491

PA.   2,122

MICH. 9,701

OHIO   1,910

W.VA.   181

VA.   2,155

N.C. 38,129

S.C.   1,098

GA.   749

KY.   391

IND.   948

ILL.   4,704

TENN.   638

ALA.   1,276

MISS. 3,119

FLA.   2,504

LA.   3,587

ARK.   580

MO.   1,723

WIS. 14,297

MINN. 15,496

IOWA   1,708

OKLA. 64,689

KANS. 5,069

TEXAS 5,750

N. DAK. 11,736

S. DAK. 25,794

NEBR. 5,545

COLO. 4,288

ARIZ. 56,255

WYO.   4,020

UTAH   6,961

N. MEX. 83,387

MONT. 21,181

IDAHO 5,231

NEV.   6,681

CALIF. 39,014

WASH. 21,076

OREG. 8,026

HAWAII   472

ALASKA 14,444

INTRODUCTION

The Indians have always been an anomaly in American history, for the red Americans did not behave as the European invaders expected. They were not absorbed or assimilated, nor did they disintegrate and disappear as predicted by whites who called the Indian the "vanishing American." There were no established norms to be applied to the relations between the two cultures that met in the region that became the United States; and Indian affairs have been a perpetual perplexity to the people of the United States and to their government. That the Indians were here first has always been something of an embarrassment to the whites; that they are still here, as strongly attached to their culture as ever and developing newer and more effective ways to make themselves heard, is one of the paradoxes of our age.

The relations between the Indians and the whites have received extensive attention from American historians but not as much as one might expect, given the centuries of contact. To many persons, indeed, the Indians in the United States have been the forgotten minority, a small remnant that history seems to have passed by. There have been periodic public outcries against the treatment accorded the Indians by the aggressive Anglo-Americans, and at the present time the reawakening consciousness among Indian groups of their heritage and place in American society is reflected in a new concern on the part of historians to study the development of Indian-white relations in America's past. But the scholarly histories have not yet reached a wide audience.

The writings, it should be noted, for the most part reflect the white man's point of view, for they are mostly by white historians and based on historical sources left by the dominant society. Only in very recent times has there been collected a notable body of materials dealing with the Indian side of the story— for example, in oral history projects which have recorded interviews with many Indians—but these resources have not yet been extensively exploited by historians. This is not to say, however, that the Indians have been treated unsympathetically, for historical works about Indian relations have given much space to the injustices the whites have worked upon the native peoples.

Three themes predominate in historical writing about the American Indians and their relations with the whites. One of these is the dispossession of the Indians, as the whites pushed relentlessly westward in search of lands to settle and resources to exploit. A second is the concerted and persistent effort to assimilate the Indians into the mainstream of white society—to break down the tribal patterns and replace them with the civilization of the Anglo-Americans—an attack upon cultural ways that came from men of a humanitarian outlook who sought to benefit the Indians. Both of these threads of historiography are represented in the readings in this book.

The third theme is the warfare between the Indians and the Anglo-Americans which marked almost three centuries of contact, from early in the seventeenth century to the end of the nineteenth. This military aspect of Indian affairs has been more thoroughly covered by historians than Indian policy in general and is better known; because of limitations of space it forms no part of this volume. We are concerned here, rather, with the evolving policies of the American government in its attempts to reach a solution to the "Indian problem," with the vacillations in policy, the pressures of humanitarian reformers as well as avaricious western frontiersmen, the work of Indian education, and the Christianizing efforts of the missionaries.

The evils in white America's treatment of the Indians have received much attention, for they were severe and easy to document. Reformers in America have usually been articulate and outspoken, and humanitarians interested in the Indians were no exception. Those who saw the callous treatment of the aborigines by the whites cried out on behalf of the victims, and a considerable literature of protest developed in the nineteenth century as well as in our own day. That it was often polemical rather than scholarly, sentimental rather than well-argued, merely increased its effect upon the popular mind and to a lesser extent upon historians, who sometimes relied upon it for their general treatment of Indian affairs.

The classic example of such writing is the work of a minor literary figure who became converted to Indian reform: Helen Hunt Jackson's *A Century of Dishonor*. Mrs. Jackson's work is a tribe-by-tribe recitation of broken treaties, unkept promises, and dishonest dealings, by which she hoped to arouse the public conscience of her day. She was not writing balanced history, but her volume has served as a rich quarry, and her viewpoint is often reflected in the works of serious scholars. American historians have by and large written in terms of an oppressed minority, dispossessed or destroyed by an aggressive and dominant Anglo-American society and its government.

An understanding of how the Christian whites could behave in such a fashion depends upon a knowledge of the views and beliefs they held about the aborigines. That the whites in the early decades of our history adopted a superior attitude toward the Indians and used that superiority to justify the inevitable disappearance of the red men is clearly shown in the important book by Roy Harvey Pearce, *Savagism and Civilization: A Study of the Indian and the American*

Mind. Pearce's book is of the genre that investigates beliefs, images, and myths, tracing their existence in the literature of the period and showing their importance for the attitudes and actions of the people who absorbed them. Although he is primarily interested in savagism as a mirror in which the whites could see reflections of themselves and their own civilization, Pearce provides a penetrating insight into the American mind as it faced the Indian.

In the light of such beliefs as Pearce depicts, it is understandable enough that the Indians would suffer at the hands of the whites, and numerous historians have described and analyzed the pushing back of the Indians. One excellent scholarly appraisal of early American Indian policy, which shows a typical view of white unconcern for Indian rights, is the article by Reginald Horsman, "American Indian Policy and the Origins of Manifest Destiny." Horsman sees a genuine sense of mission among Americans and their statesmen, who looked upon white expansion as a means of bringing to the Indians the blessings of civilization, but he notes that "the American government used military force, bribery, deception, and every other possible means to expand the arc of American expansion." He concludes that the common assumption was that "the suffering of whoever stood in the way of expansion was nothing beside the benefit to humanity of extending the area of American civilization and freedom." Action against the Indians conditioned the United States for later expansion against other hapless peoples.

The one series of events in the first half of the nineteenth century that has become the touchstone for historians' condemnation of the federal government's Indian policy was Indian removal. The moving in the 1820s and 1830s of the eastern tribes—especially the Five Civilized Tribes of the southeastern United States—from their ancestral homes to new lands west of the Mississippi has often been interpreted as the unmistakable indication that Indian rights would not be protected against land-hungry whites. A notable example of this viewpoint is provided in Dale Van Every's *Disinherited: The Lost Birthright of the American Indian.* Although not a work of original scholarly research, the book in excellent style tells the tragic story of the removal of the Cherokees and of their "Trail of Tears" to the West, drawing skillfully upon contemporary writing engendered by the removal policy.

The harsh views of American beliefs and actions in the dispossessing of the Indians have not gone completely unchallenged. Although recognizing the truth of many of the charges made, some recent historians have questioned the overall validity of the interpretations. They have taken a new look at the evidence and put forward new interpretations. These historians are not numerous enough or unified enough in their views to be considered a "revisionist school," but they question the traditional conclusions and point to what they consider genuinely humane aspects of the official policies. They note also the problems facing the federal government and find good points as well as bad in the proposals and programs; and they are concerned with understanding what happens when diverse cultures meet and intermingle. That such an approach is not entirely new is evident from the brief appendix of Theodore Roosevelt's *Winning of the West,* in which, before the turn of the century, he took issue with writers who had too dim a view of governmental actions.

A historian who has restudied early Puritan treatment of the Indians is Alden T. Vaughan. His *New England Frontier: Puritans and Indians, 1620–1675* investigates the relations between the two races before King Philip's War. In his conclusion Vaughan bluntly states his disagreement with previous interpretations. He finds, not "a clash of dissimilar ways of life, but rather the expansion of one into the areas in which the other was lacking." Another student of Indian-white relations in early America is Bernard W. Sheehan. His review essay in the *William and Mary Quarterly* is ostensibly an appraisal of books and articles dealing with the subject, but it is also a statement of his own views. He criticizes the "simplistic duality" between helpless Indian and brazen white man, which "makes the assignment of guilt an easy task." Instead he sees the conflict "submerged in the process of cultural intermingling"—a condition that makes a moralistic laying of blame a very difficult thing.

More clearly revisionist in approach is Francis Paul Prucha's essay, "Andrew Jackson's Indian Policy: A Reassessment." Andrew Jackson, the great villain of Indian removal and dispossession in the minds of many, is shown to be less harshly inclined toward the Indians than has been traditionally held. In the light of the real and difficult problems facing the statesmen of Jackson's era, especially in the conflict between the Indian nations and the eastern states, the removal policy is seen as a reasonable solution, not simply as ruthless aggression.

The next group of readings deals with the attempts to assimilate the Indians into white society. In the ethnocentric view of the Anglo-Americans, who were absolutely convinced of the superiority of their Christian civilization to what they considered the pagan savagism of the Indians, there could be only one ultimate outcome. The Indians would be raised from their benighted condition, accept the goals and virtues of the whites, and be assimilated into the white society. Although some men questioned the ability of the Indians to make this change and predicted their early disappearance, many Americans dealing with the red men were convinced of the possibility of acculturation and worked with might and main to bring it about. Until well into the twentieth century the work of the government agents, the zeal of the missionaries, and the hopes and dreams of the humanitarian reformers all moved toward the same goal, the transformation of the Indians into white Americans.

Historians and anthropologists have studied the attempts at assimilation with some care, tracing the historical developments toward acculturation and critically evaluating the results. In *Salvation and the Savage,* Robert F. Berkhofer, Jr., writes about the Christianizing and civilizing efforts of Protestant missionaries up to 1862. The missionaries were among the principal agents devoted consciously to changing the Indian ways into patterns of white society. Since their goals were also in large part the goals of the government agents, Berkhofer's analysis of the objects of the missionaries tells us a great deal about white policies in general. And the failure of the missionaries' efforts, growing out of their inability to see and appreciate the differences between the culture of the Indian and that of the white man, helps us understand the persistence of Indian culture to our own day.

A climax in the movement toward Indian acculturation—called "Indian reform" by its sponsors—came with the Dawes Act of 1887, which provided for the distribution of Indian lands in severalty. Only when individual ownership replaced communal tribal ownership, it was argued, could the Indians become true citizens and enjoy fully the benefits of white civilization. Loring Benson Priest's study of this post-Civil War "reformation of United States Indian policy," *Uncle Sam's Stepchildren,* is a careful analysis of the changes in policy and their effects. Priest considers the Dawes Act "the most significant step taken to aid the red man since the formation of the Republic," and he laments its failure; "misapplication by administrators rather than the evil intent of legislators," he argues, "was responsible for the disastrous history of America's first systematic effort to provide for Indian welfare."

The failures of the severalty act—primarily the loss of Indian land as the individual holdings were quickly alienated—led to a reversal of the policy in the 1930s. A return to tribal ownership and a renewal of emphasis on Indian culture came during John Collier's administration as Commissioner of Indian Affairs from 1933 to 1945. The philosophy and goals of this "Indian New Deal" are described by Collier himself in his 1947 book, *Indians of the Americas.* Collier's position was not without its critics, who saw in a return to Indian ways a repudiation of the long decades of labor to assimilate the Indians, but ever since his time it has been difficult to disregard the Indians' own outlook and desires in planning Indian policy. And that the Indians in fact have not been acculturated but hold strongly to their own cultural ways is becoming increasingly evident. One able statement, a summing up of much anthropological work, is Evon Z. Vogt's article, "The Acculturation of American Indians." Vogt offers explanations why after long years of attempted assimilation the Indians have not been incorporated but are still a distinct cultural group.

If the Indians then are here to stay, what is to be their position in American society? Ethnic minorities are developing a new consciousness, a new appreciation of their special heritage, an interest in their historical experience in America, and a demand for recognition of their rights and dignity. Part of this phenomenon is the reawakening of Indian groups and a pan-Indianism with some overtones of "red power." Much of the writing on Indian rights is strident in tone, and the agitation is too recent to permit careful historical evaluation. A reasonable approach toward understanding the Indians in the present-day United

States, however, is that of Edward H. Spicer, an anthropologist with deep historical insights. His *A Short History of the Indians of the United States* is an attempt to see the Indians' history from the standpoint of their own society, not primarily from the viewpoint of adjustment to the white society's aims and institutions. Spicer emphasizes the continuity of Indian groups and the transformations they have made, and in the end he describes the state of Indian nationalism today.

The final selection in the book illustrates the Indians' demands to have a hand in planning their own future. Vine Deloria, Jr., a Sioux Indian with extensive education, became involved as a spokesman for Indian rights as director of the National Congress of American Indians. In his article "The War Between the Redskins and the Feds," in the *New York Times Magazine,* he describes the Indian opposition to Secretary of the Interior Walter Hickel and traces briefly the history of injustices to the Indian. He ends with a strong assertion of recent Indian progress and a plea that white America listen to and learn from the Indian tribes.

As Indians come more and more into the consciousness of the nation, they will begin to get more attention from historians. New Indian sources will be added to the accumulation of sources derived from records kept by whites, and new analyses by both Indians and non-Indians will deepen our accurate understanding of this enduring part of the history of the United States. But questions, old and new, will continue to face Americans. How have the special relationships between Indian tribes and the government set Indians apart from other minority groups in the United States? Is eventual assimilation of Indians into the cultural patterns of white Americans a feasible and worthy goal? Do current proposals on Indian affairs arise from a desire to make up for genuine injustices in the past? Or have historians overemphasized the injustices at the expense of a fundamental understanding of the intercultural problems that faced the United States? What lessons can the present-day United States learn from the Indians and their historical experience?

Divergent viewpoints and challenging historical interpretations will sharpen our appreciation of the complexities of Indian-white relations and will, hopefully, bring us the wisdom we need to answer the questions in a spirit of sympathy and justice.

In the reprinted selections footnotes appearing in the original sources have in general been omitted unless they contribute to the argument or better understanding of the selection.

A Century of Dishonor is the classic statement of American injustice to the Indians. Written in 1881 by HELEN HUNT JACKSON (1830–1885), a minor poet and novelist, the book was intended to stir up the public conscience, and the author at her own expense sent a copy of the book to every member of Congress. The bulk of the book is a tribe-by-tribe recitation of dispossession, broken treaties, and callous disregard of rights. As such, it is a one-sided and emotional tract, hardly to be taken as a fair appraisal. Yet its message fell upon sympathetic ears, and the "century of dishonor" approach has played a prominent part in historical writings about Indian-white relations in the United States. The brief selections printed below, taken from the beginning and the end of the book, give the essence of the author's plea. Can this type of writing serve a useful purpose?*

Helen Hunt Jackson

A Century of Dishonor

The history of the United States Government's repeated violations of faith with the Indians . . . convicts us, as a nation, not only of having outraged the principles of justice, which are the basis of international law; and of having laid ourselves open to the accusation of both cruelty and perfidy; but of having made ourselves liable to all punishments which follow upon such sins—to arbitrary punishment at the hands of any civilized nation who might see fit to call us to account, and to that more certain natural punishment which, sooner or later, as surely comes from evil-doing as harvests come from sown seed.

To prove all this it is only necessary to study the history of any one of the Indian tribes. I propose to give in the following chapters merely outline sketches of the history of a few of them, not entering more into details than is necessary to show the repeated broken faith of the United States Government toward them. A full history of the wrongs they have suffered at the hands of the authorities, military and civil, and also of the citizens of this country, it would take years to write and volumes to hold.

There is but one hope of righting this wrong. It lies in appeal to the heart and conscience of the American people. What the people demand, Congress will do. It has been—to our shame be it spoken—at the demand of part of the people that all these wrongs have been committed,

*From Helen Hunt Jackson, *A Century of Dishonor: A Sketch of the United States Government's Dealings with Some of the Indian Tribes* (New York: Harper & Brothers, 1881), pp. 29–31, 336–342.

these treaties broken, these robberies done, by the Government.

So long as there remains on our frontier one square mile of land occupied by a weak and helpless owner, there will be a strong and unscrupulous frontiersman ready to seize it, and a weak and unscrupulous politician, who can be hired for a vote or for money, to back him.

The only thing that can stay this is a mighty outspoken sentiment and purpose of the great body of the people. Right sentiment and right purpose in a Senator here and there, and a Representative here and there, are little more than straws which make momentary eddies, but do not obstruct the tide. The precedents of a century's unhindered and profitable robbery have mounted up into a very Gibraltar of defence and shelter to those who care for nothing but safety and gain. That such precedents should be held, and openly avowed as standards, is only one more infamy added to the list. Were such logic employed in the case of an individual man, how quick would all men see its enormity. Suppose that a man had had the misfortune to be born into a family whose name had been blackened by generations of criminals; that his father, his grandfather, and his great-grandfather before them had lived in prisons, and died on scaffolds, should that man say in his soul, "Go to! What is the use? I also will commit robbery and murder, and get the same gain by it which my family must have done?" Or shall he say in his soul, "God help me! I will do what may be within the power of one man, and the compass of one generation, to atone for the wickedness, and to make clean the name of my dishonored house!"

What an opportunity for the Congress of 1880 to cover itself with a lustre of glory, as the first to cut short our nation's record of cruelties and perjuries! the first to attempt to redeem the name of the United States from the stain of a century of dishonor! . . .

There are within the limits of the United States between two hundred and fifty and three hundred thousand Indians, exclusive of those in Alaska. The names of the different tribes and bands, as entered in the statistical tables of the Indian Office Reports, number nearly three hundred. One of the most careful estimates which has been made of their numbers and localities gives them as follows: "In Minnesota and States east of the Mississippi, about 32,500; in Nebraska, Kansas, and the Indian Territory, 70,650; in the Territories of Dakota, Montana, Wyoming, and Idaho, 65,000; in Nevada and the Territories of Colorado, New Mexico, Utah, and Arizona, 84,000; and on the Pacific slope, 48,000."

Of these, 130,000 are self-supporting on their own reservations, "receiving nothing from the Government except interest on their own moneys, or annuities granted them in consideration of the cession of their lands to the United States."

This fact alone would seem sufficient to dispose forever of the accusation, so persistently brought against the Indian, that he will not work.

Of the remainder, 84,000 are partially supported by the Government—the interest money due them and their annuities, as provided by treaty, being inadequate to their subsistence on the reservations where they are confined. In many cases, however, these Indians furnish a large part of their support—the White River Utes, for instance, who are reported by the Indian Bureau as getting sixty-six per cent of their living by "root-digging, hunting, and fishing"; the Squaxin band, in Washington Territory, as earning seventy-five per cent, and the

Chippewas of Lake Superior as earning fifty per cent in the same way. These facts also would seem to dispose of the accusation that the Indian will not work.

There are about 55,000 who never visit an agency, over whom the Government does not pretend to have either control or care. These 55,000 "subsist by hunting, fishing, on roots, nuts, berries, etc., and by begging and stealing"; and this also seems to dispose of the accusation that the Indian will not "work for a living." There remains a small portion, about 31,000, that are entirely subsisted by the Government.

There is not among these three hundred bands of Indians one which has not suffered cruelly at the hands either of the Government or of white settlers. The poorer, the more insignificant, the more helpless the band, the more certain the cruelty and outrage to which they have been subjected. This is especially true of the bands on the Pacific slope. These Indians found themselves of a sudden surrounded by and caught up in the great influx of gold-seeking settlers, as helpless creatures on a shore are caught up in a tidal wave. There was not time for the Government to make treaties; not even time for communities to make laws. The tale of the wrongs, the oppressions, the murders of the Pacific-slope Indians in the last thirty years would be a volume by itself, and is too monstrous to be believed.

It makes little difference, however, where one opens the record of the history of the Indians; every page and every year has its dark stain. The story of one tribe is the story of all, varied only by differences of time and place; but neither time nor place makes any difference in the main facts. Colorado is as greedy and unjust in 1880 as was Georgia in 1830, and Ohio in 1795; and the United States Government breaks promises now as

deftly as then, and with an added ingenuity from long practice.

One of its strongest supports in so doing is the wide-spread sentiment among the people of dislike to the Indian, of impatience with his presence as a "barrier to civilization," and distrust of it as a possible danger. The old tales of the frontier life, with its horrors of Indian warfare, have gradually, by two or three generations' telling, produced in the average mind something like an hereditary instinct of unquestioning and unreasoning aversion which it is almost impossible to dislodge or soften.

There are hundreds of pages of unimpeachable testimony on the side of the Indian; but it goes for nothing, is set down as sentimentalism or partisanship, tossed aside and forgotten.

President after president has appointed commission after commission to inquire into and report upon Indian affairs, and to make suggestions as to the best methods of managing them. The reports are filled with eloquent statements of wrongs done to the Indians, of perfidies on the part of the Government; they counsel, as earnestly as words can, a trial of the simple and unperplexing expedients of telling truth, keeping promises, making fair bargains, dealing justly in all ways and all things. These reports are bound up with the Government's Annual Reports, and that is the end of them. It would probably be no exaggeration to say that not one American citizen out of ten thousand ever sees them or knows that they exist, and yet any one of them, circulated throughout the country, read by the right-thinking, right-feeling men and women of this land, would be of itself a "campaign document" that would initiate a revolution which would not subside until the Indians' wrongs were, so far as is now left possible, righted.

In 1869 President Grant appointed a commission of nine men, representing the influence and philanthropy of six leading States, to visit the different Indian reservations, and to "examine all matters appertaining to Indian affairs."

In the report of this commission are such paragraphs as the following:

"To assert that 'the Indian will not work' is as true as it would be to say that the white man will not work.

"Why should the Indian be expected to plant corn, fence lands, build houses, or do anything but get food from day to day, when experience has taught him that the product of his labor will be seized by the white man to-morrow? The most industrious white man would become a drone under similar circumstances. Nevertheless, many of the Indians" (the commissioners might more forcibly have said 130,000 of the Indians) "are already at work, and furnish ample refutation of the assertion that 'the Indian will not work.' There is no escape from the inexorable logic of facts.

"The history of the Government connections with the Indians is a shameful record of broken treaties and unfulfilled promises. The history of the border white man's connection with the Indians is a sickening record of murder, outrage, robbery, and wrongs committed by the former, as the rule, and occasional savage outbreaks and unspeakably barbarous deeds of retaliation by the latter, as the exception.

"Taught by the Government that they had rights entitled to respect, when those rights have been assailed by the rapacity of the white man, the arm which should have been raised to protect them has ever been ready to sustain the aggressor.

"The testimony of some of the highest military officers of the United States is on record to the effect that, in our Indian wars, almost without exception, the first aggressions have been made by the white man; and the assertion is supported by every civilian of reputation who has studied the subject. In addition to the class of robbers and outlaws who find impunity in their nefarious pursuits on the frontiers, there is a large class of professedly reputable men who use every means in their power to bring on Indian wars for the sake of the profit to be realized from the presence of troops and the expenditure of Government funds in their midst. They proclaim death to the Indians at all times in words and publications, making no distinction between the innocent and the guilty. They incite the lowest class of men to the perpetration of the darkest deeds against their victims, and as judges and jurymen shield them from the justice due to their crimes. Every crime committed by a white man against an Indian is concealed or palliated. Every offence committed by an Indian against a white man is borne on the wings of the post or the telegraph to the remotest corner of the land, clothed with all the horrors which the reality or imagination can throw around it. Against such influences as these the people of the United States need to be warned."

To assume that it would be easy, or by any one sudden stroke of legislative policy possible, to undo the mischief and hurt of the long past, set the Indian policy of the country right for the future, and make the Indians at once safe and happy, is the blunder of a hasty and uninformed judgment. The notion which seems to be growing more prevalent, that simply to make all Indians at once citizens of the United States would be a sovereign and instantaneous panacea for all their ills and all the Government's perplexities, is a very inconsiderate one. To administer complete citizenship of a sudden, all round, to all Indians, barbarous and civilized alike, would be as grotesque a blunder as to dose them all round with any one medicine, irrespective of the symptoms and needs of their diseases. It would kill more than it would cure. Nevertheless, it is true, as was well stated by one of the superintendents of Indian Affairs in 1857, that, "so long as they are not citizens of the United States, their rights of property must remain insecure against invasion. The doors of the federal tribunals being barred against them while wards and dependents, they can only partially exercise the rights of free government, or give to those who make, execute, and construe the few laws they are allowed to enact, dignity sufficient to make them respectable. While they continue individually to gather the crumbs that fall from the table of the United States, idleness, improvidence, and indebtedness will be the rule, and industry, thrift, and freedom from debt the exception. The utter absence of individual title to particular lands deprives every one among them of the chief incentive to labor and exertion —the very mainspring on which the prosperity of a people depends."

All judicious plans and measures for their safety and salvation must embody provisions for their becoming citizens as fast as they are fit, and must protect them till then in every right and particular in which our laws protect other "persons" who are not citizens.

There is a disposition in a certain class of minds to be impatient with any protestation against wrong which is unaccompanied or unprepared with a quick and exact scheme of remedy. This is illogical. When pioneers in a new country find a tract of poisonous and swampy wilderness to be reclaimed, they do not withhold their hands from fire and axe till they see clearly which way roads should run, where good water will spring, and what crops will best grow on the redeemed land. They first clear the swamp. So with this poisonous and baffling part of the domain of our national affairs—let us first "clear the swamp."

However great perplexity and difficulty there may be in the details of any and every plan possible for doing at this late day anything like justice to the Indian, however hard it may be for good statesmen and good men to agree upon the things that ought to be done, there certainly is, or ought to be, no perplexity whatever, no difficulty whatever, in agreeing upon certain things that ought not to be done, and which must cease to be done before the first steps can be taken toward righting the wrongs, curing the ills, and wiping out the disgrace to us of the present condition of our Indians.

Cheating, robbing, breaking promises —these three are clearly things which must cease to be done. One more thing, also, and that is the refusal of the protection of the law to the Indian's rights of property, "of life, liberty, and the pursuit of happiness."

When these four things have ceased to be done, time, statesmanship, philanthropy, and Christianity can slowly and surely do the rest. Till these four things have ceased to be done, statesmanship and philanthropy alike must work in vain, and even Christianity can reap but small harvest.

The intellectual climate in which Indian policy was formulated is the subject of a fascinating book, published in 1953, by ROY HARVEY PEARCE (b. 1919), who is now professor of American literature at the University of California at San Diego. *Savagism and Civilization: A Study of the Indian and the American Mind* is, the author says, "a book about a belief." It treats of the American idea of civilization, a belief that was often defined negatively in terms of the savage Indians, who as obstacles to progress forced Americans to consider what it meant to be civilized. How can this detailed analysis of what the whites thought about the Indians help us to understand the rationalizations used to justify inevitable destruction of the Indians?*

Roy Harvey Pearce

A Melancholy Fact:
The Indian in American Life

Americans who were setting out to make a new society could find a place in it for the Indian only if he would become what they were—settled, steady, civilized. Yet somehow he would not be anything but what he was—roaming, unreliable, savage. So they concluded that they were destined to try to civilize him and, in trying, to destroy him, because he could not and would not be civilized. He was to be pitied for this, and also to be censured. Pity and censure were the price Americans would have to pay for destroying the Indian. Pity and censure would be, in the long run, the price of the progress of civilization over savagism.

Fighting a Revolution, barely able to handle the British, Americans hoped to neutralize the Indian's power and to settle with him later. The British, on their side, tried to convince him that a victory for land-hungry colonials would mean the end of his way of life. British agents and administrators were skilled in handling Indians; they guaranteed continued preservation of Indian territory, rights, and trade; their appeals were powerful, direct, and realistic. The result was that on most fronts colonial Americans found themselves troubled by Indians allied with the British. They managed to put down the British-manipulated Cherokee uprising in 1776, to withstand repeated British-encouraged frontier raids, even to attack the Indians on their own, as in Sullivan's 1779 expedition to destroy the corn and villages of Iroquois loyal to the British.

They also came to recognize that the Indian's power could never be simply neutralized, and that they would soon have to settle with him once and for all.

The Indian's fortune after the Revolution was to learn that he had no right to exist independently and to live as and where he pleased. The official American view was still the British colonial view: that Indian land was to be considered as conquered territory. Yet Indians, in the 1780's encouraged by British agents operating from British-held territory in the north and south, firmly held that their land belonged to them and must be purchased outright. Treaties were made, and boundaries were set by the new American government; and treaties were promptly broken and boundaries disregarded by frontier citizens who had little respect for their government and less for what Hugh Henry Brackenridge termed in 1782 "the animals, vulgarly called Indians."

This was to be the abiding relationship between red Indians and white Americans. In the settled east, where Indians had been done away with, it was hoped that their western lands could gradually be taken over and that they might as gradually be civilized and absorbed into the oncoming white population. Congress acted toward this end in 1786 when it placed control of Indian affairs solely in the hands of the national government. Yet individual states, needing to grab land, continued to treat with Indians and to get what they could; and individual frontiersmen took what they found worth taking. The Northwest Ordinance of 1787 and the Constitution of 1789 set forth an Indian policy whose central tenet was that Indian title to western land, even though it be conquered land, had to be extinguished formally before Americans might move onto it and that, further, Indians were to be settled on farms and to be civ-

ilized as their lands were taken over. Impatient frontiersmen broke the law while they forced Indians to obey it.

There was no time to civilize. Americans moving westward in effect forced the Indians to try, however vainly, to hold on to those ways of savage life which civilizing theoretically would end. Encouraged by the British, tribes in the Ohio country went so far as to repudiate early treaties with the United States and to insist that all land west of the Ohio was to be theirs forever. Desperately strong in their determination to survive, they were able to defeat the punitive expeditions of Harmar in 1790 and of St. Clair in 1791, but were completely routed by Wayne's army in 1794. At the resulting Treaty of Greenville in 1795, deserted by the British, they surrendered almost all of the Ohio country. In the southeast, tribes led by the Creeks were encouraged by Spain to resist the onrush of the pioneers of the new republic. Yet by 1790 they too were willing to accept by treaty the rule of the United States.

Treaties meant little to pioneering Americans, who moved without hesitation onto Indian lands and took what they pleased. When, for example, representatives of Kickapoos, Weas, and Delawares refused in 1802 to cede further land to the Territory of Indiana, its Governor, William Henry Harrison, informed them that the lands already belonged to the United States and would be taken over by force if necessary. Actions like Harrison's, implementing the frontier drive to land, power, and elbow room, again pushed Indians in the northwest into united resistance, this time under Tecumseh and his half brother, the Prophet. Even with British help, this attempt to resist American encroachment failed too; the final defeat of the northwest Indians became only one incident in the War of 1812. Likewise in the War of 1812, Creeks in the southeast, allied with the British once more, were put down by Andrew Jackson and his Indian haters. One of the sovereignties finally achieved in the War of 1812 was that of American over Indian. A Fourth of July toast (the tenth of the evening) drunk by officers in Sullivan's expedition in 1779 had expressed essentially what was to be proved a great and eternal frontier truth: "Civilization or death to all American Savages."

Theoretically, death was to be by the attrition rising out of gradual, ordered, intelligently-controlled expansion westward. The process, it was fully granted, would be painful but nonetheless necessary. Early it achieved official, formal recognition, so that in 1789 Henry Knox, Secretary of War and thus in charge of Indian affairs, could serenely declare:

> Although the disposition of the people of the States, to emigrate into the Indian country, cannot be effectually prevented, it may be restrained and regulated.
>
> It may be restrained, by postponing new purchases of Indian territory, and by prohibiting the citizens from intruding on the Indian lands.
>
> In may be regulated, by forming colonies, under the direction of Government, and by posting a body of troops to execute their orders.
>
> As population shall increase, and approach the Indian boundaries, game will be diminished, and new purchases may be made for small considerations. This has been, and probably will be, the inevitable consequence of cultivation.
>
> It is, however, painful to consider, that all the Indian tribes, once existing in those States now the best cultivated and most populous, have become extinct. If the same causes continue, the same effects will happen; and, in a short period, the idea of an Indian on this side the Mississippi will only be found in the page of the historian.

Actually, death was more violent than Knox had planned. The Louisiana Purchase of 1803 made it possible to conceive of removing Indians to a place where they would be out of civilization's way, where they might have a chance to survive as savages, where they even might be brought to wished-for civilization. This was to be west of the Mississippi on land which no civilized man would ever covet. The conception seems to have been part of Jefferson's intention in arranging the Purchase. It was, in any case, an obvious solution to a worrisome problem and was hopefully entertained by both friends and enemies of the Indian, the former glad to have a means of keeping him out of harm's way, the latter glad to be rid of him. When the clash of Indian and white on the frontier finally demanded it, in the 1820's and 30's, the conception was realized formally as the government's policy of Removal, whereby Indians east of the Mississippi would trade lands needed by civilized men for western lands more suited to savage use. First, beginning in 1825, Indians in the northwest country were maneuvered into ceding their lands and removing to the Indian Territory, west of the 95th meridian; the only violent resistance, that of Black Hawk and the Sauks and Foxes, was ruthlessly beaten down. Then in 1830 the southeastern Indians began moving west at the request of the government, and in ten years had almost all made new homes in the Territory. Of the southeastern Indians, only the eastern Cherokees, even then settled on farms and asking for citizenship, tried to assert their American rights. Their resistance was beaten down when in 1838 troops marched them from Georgia to their new home in the west; six months on the way, they lost by death on the march about one-tenth of their number. Such resistance and such an end to it made one thing clear: Indians could be considered only as charity cases, victims inevitably of the law of civilized progress.

President Jackson summed up the matter for his fellow Americans in his Second Annual Message, December 6, 1830:

Humanity has often wept over the fate of the aborigines of this country, and Philanthropy has been long busily employed in devising means to avert it, but its progress has never for a moment been arrested, and one by one have many powerful tribes disappeared from the earth. To follow to the tomb the last of his race and to tread on the graves of extinct nations excite melancholy reflections. But true philanthropy reconciles the mind to these vicissitudes as it does to the extinction of one generation to make room for another. . . . Philanthropy could not wish to see this continent restored to the condition in which it was found by our forefathers. What good man would prefer a country covered with forests and ranged by a few thousand savages to our extensive Republic, studded with cities, towns, and prosperous farms, embellished with all the improvements which art can devise or industry execute, occupied by more than 12,000,000 happy people, and filled with all the blessings of liberty, civilization and religion?

The present policy of the Government is but a continuation of the same progressive change by a milder process. . . .

Thus mildly and progressively the Indian exchanged his home east of the Mississippi for one west and was forced out of American life into American history. . . .

Americans had always felt that the process of acculturation, of throwing off one way of life for another, would be relatively simple. To be civilized the Indian would have merely to be made into a farmer; this was a matter of an education for a generation or two. Christianization would follow inevitably; perhaps Christianization itself was the way to civilization. But acculturation was not a simple process, as we know now, at least. For a culture is a delicately balanced system of attitudes, beliefs, valuations, conditions, and modes of behavior; the system does not change and reintegrate itself overnight, or in a generation or two. This is what those Americans who were trying to civilize the Indians inevitably discovered, although they did not know it precisely as this. Civilized, Christian life did not raise up all savages as it should have. Rather it lowered some savages and destroyed others. This was the melancholy fact which Americans understood as coming inevitably in the progress of civilization over savagism.

The basis of their understanding had long been part of the grand rationale of westward-moving colonialism. This was the tradition of the natural and divine superiority of a farming to a hunting culture. Universally Americans could see the Indian only as hunter. That his culture, at least the culture of the eastern Indians whom they knew best until the second quarter of the nineteenth century, was as much agrarian as hunting, they simply could not see. They forgot too, if they had ever known, that many of their own farming methods had been taken over directly from the Indians whom they were pushing westward. One can say only that their intellectual and cultural traditions, their idea of order, so informed their thoughts and their actions that they could see and conceive of nothing but the Indian who hunted.

Biblical injunction framed their belief; and on the frontier practical conditions supported it. The Indian with his known hunting ways needed many square miles on which to live, whereas the white farmer needed only a few acres. The latter way was obviously more economical and intelligent; it was essentially the civilized way. Therefore the Indian would have to move on to make way for a better and higher life. If the Indian's fate was a sad one and civilized men should be properly moved by it, still, in the long run, the prospects were exciting and ennobling. Thus an historian towards the end of the eighteenth century:

The Savage has his day; and enjoys life according to the taste and habits he possesses; he casts his eyes abroad, over the extensive wilderness of his wild domain, and sighs at the apprehension that his nation and race must cease to exist, and that his mighty forests must finally bow to human strength; and that the hills and vallies, where he has enjoyed the chase, shall be covered with cities and cultivated fields of white men. His agonies, at first, seem to demand a tear from the eye of humanity; but when we reflect, that the extinction of his race, and the progress of the arts which give rise to his distressing apprehensions, are for the increase of mankind, and for the promotion of the world's glory and happiness; that five hundred rational animals may enjoy life in plenty, and comfort, where only one Savage drags out a hungry existence, we shall be pleased with the perspective into futurity.

Yet belief in the glorious possibilities of a culture built out of cities and cultivated fields was based on something more than Biblical injunction and economic necessity. "Those who labor in the earth," Jefferson had written in 1784, "are the chosen people of God, if ever He had a chosen people. Whose breasts He has made His peculiar deposit for substantial and genuine virtue." This is agrarian idealism, the belief that men, having a natural right to their land by occupation and labor, achieve status and dignity by exercising that right and becoming freeholding farmers. It is a deep-rooted belief, whose theoretical ground derives from the Lockean theory of the free individual and the metaphysics and sociology of his freedom. For Locke—and virtually all Americans were, in the most general sense, Lockeans—man achieved his highest humanity by taking something out of nature and converting it with his labor

into part of himself. His private property, conceived of in terms of the close, personal relationships of an agrarian society, was his means to social maturity. It gave him stability, self-respect, privacy, and the basis for civilized society itself. For Americans the Lockean theory must have made savage society seem loose, immature, virtually anarchic, full of the false freedom of doing as one pleased; likewise, for Americans the theory now must have made it all the more possible to see how Indians could become truly rational animals. All, indeed, that an Indian would need to be on his way to civilization was, in the words of the Secretary of War in 1789, "a love for exclusive property."

Through the end of the eighteenth century and well into the nineteenth, this theme was worked over by Americans who, trying to understand what was happening to the Indian, wanted to make sense of their feeling of pity and censure. The revolutionary General and political figure, Benjamin Lincoln, addressed a scholarly letter on the matter to the historian Jeremy Belknap, January 21, 1792. He laid down a general principle:

Civilized and uncivilized people cannot live in the same territory, or even in the same neighborhood. Civilization directs us to remove as fast as possible that natural growth from the lands which is absolutely essential for the food and hiding-place to those beasts of the forests upon which the uncivilized principally depend for support.

Lincoln pleaded for fair and honest treatment of Indians who constituted the uncivilized of America. Yet, he had to conclude, ". . . the time will come when they will be either civilized or extinct."

The matter was immediate and personal to Lincoln. Journeying to an Indian treaty at Detroit in 1793, he could see civilized agrarian power as divinely ordained. On July 14, on Lake Erie, he surveyed the landscape lovingly and rhapsodized in his journal:

When I take a view of this extensive country, and contemplate the clemency of its seasons, the richness of its soil, see the saccharine, so grateful to our tastes, and necessary perhaps, from habit, to our happiness, flowing from the trees of the forest; and observe the fountains of salt water, and spots of earth impregnated with saline particles, called salt-licks, to which the beasts resort, from the former of which a full supply of salt can be drawn for all the inhabitants at a very moderate price, while their situation is so far inland as to make this article, important to the well-being of man and beast, too expensive to be obtained in any other way; when I farther consider the many natural advantages, if not peculiar to yet possessed by this country, and that it is capable of giving support to an hundred times as many inhabitants as now occupy it (for there is at present little more to be seen on the greatest proportion of the lands than here and there the footstep of the savage,) I cannot persuade myself that it will remain long in so uncultivated a state; especially, when I consider that to people fully this earth was in the original plan of the benevolent Deity. I am confident that sooner or later there will be a full accomplishment of the original system; and that no men will be suffered to live by hunting on lands capable of improvement, and which would support more people under a state of cultivation. So that if the savages cannot be civilized and quit their present pursuits, they will, in consequence of their stubbornness, dwindle and moulder away, from causes perhaps imperceptible to us, until the whole race shall become extinct, or they shall have reached those climes about the great lakes, where, from the rocks and the mountainous state, the footsteps of the husbandman will not be seen.

As extinction of the Indian seemed more and more a likelihood, analyses like Lincoln's came more and more to furnish a basis for understanding what was happening. When the eastern Cherokees were praised in the 1830's, it was primarily because they were farmers and thus on the way to high civilization. For all explanations of the essential weaknesses of savage society had as a basic tenet the assumption that Indians were not farmers, and all plans for civilizing Indians assumed they needed to be farmers. Jefferson, a realist who believed that Indians would have to be crushed so long as they made trouble on the frontier, again and again advised his Indian subjects to accept the white man's farming ways, so to improve themselves. As he addressed the Potawatomis in 1802:

[The] resources [of farming] are certain: they will never disappoint you: while those of hunting may fail, and expose your women and children to the miseries of hunger and cold. We will with pleasure furnish you with implements for the most necessary arts, and with persons who may instruct you how to make use of them.

Even General Jackson, as a practicing Indian-hater, wrote President Monroe from his Tennessee headquarters, March 4, 1817, "Their existence and happiness now depend upon a change in their habits and customs. . . ."

Much of the Congressional debate over the Removal policy in the 1820's and 30's centered on legalistic problems rising from the relationship between farming and hunting societies. The text for such debates most often was Vattel's classic Law of Nations, the standard American authority for international law. Vattel had considered the colonization of America and had written:

The whole earth is destined to furnish sustenance for its inhabitants; but it can not do this unless it be cultivated. Every nation is therefore bound by the natural law to cultivate the land which has fallen to its share, and it has no right to extend its boundaries or to obtain help from other Nations except in so far as the land it inhabits can not supply its needs. . . . Those who still pursue this idle [i.e., hunting] mode of life occupy more land than they would have need of under a system of honest labor, and they may not complain if other more industrious Nations, too confined at home, should come and occupy part of their lands. Thus, while the conquest of the civilized Empires of Peru and Mexico was a notorious usurpation, the establishment of various colonies upon the continent of North America might, if done within just limits, have been entirely lawful. The peoples of those vast tracts of land rather roamed over them than inhabited them.

Seventeenth-century dependence upon Genesis had shifted to nineteenth-century dependence upon natural law. American progress could be rationalized and comprehended in predominantly naturalistic terms. The Indian's way and its fatal weakness could be placed in intelligible relationship to the white man's way and its glorious strength. Westward civilized destiny was clearly manifest even in the state of the savages who were about to die.

Thus the history of American relations with the Indians came to make orderly sense. For the law of nations might be squared with the civilized morality which developed out of the sense of private property, and these in turn with the facts of westward-moving American life. During the final years of the controversy over Removal, the western lawyer, journalist, and novelist, James Hall, set out to survey the history of "Intercourse of the American People with the Indians" in just such terms. His view is standard, even hackneyed.

The history of Indian-American relations is for Hall one of mistakes, misconceptions, and mistreatment. Indians, good in their simple fashion, had welcomed Europeans peacably. Europeans had treated them as though they were sovereign nations but had not really believed that they were. There followed inevitably

encroachment on Indian lands, Indian hatred, Indian retaliation, the barbarism and viciousness of savage warfare, and always Indian defeat. Proper treatment and a policy of separation would have meant gradual civilization and Christianization. But the terrible drive of Americans westward and their inability to keep themselves from taking over Indian lands had resulted only in converting Indian virtues into Indian vices and had necessitated Removal and its consequences of disease and degradation.

But, Hall argues, what is past is past. Indians are no longer simple and straightforward in their savage goodness, but degenerate. The question is now: "How shall we deal with a people, between whom and ourselves, there is no community of language, thought, or custom —no reciprocity of obligations—no common standard, by which to estimate our relative interests, claims and duties?" How, in short, shall we deal with a people with whom we have almost completely lost cultural contact? How shall we close the gap between savage life and civilized? Can it, in fact, be closed? Studying the record of Indian-white relations in America, Hall can pose his questions only in those terms which have made them, terms involving, above all, the theory of the hunting versus the farming culture and of the virtues of civilized systems of private land tenure.

Moreover, he can answer only in such terms. The savages are a "wandering horde" and have no sense of property, therefore no laws, therefore no government. It follows that they have not the rights which a properly integrated people or organized government could claim. Yet in this age of "liberal thought, free principles, and the dissemination of knowledge," Americans have a duty, as it were, to "create" rights for the savages.

"To come at once to the point, we believe that it is the duty of our government, to take the Indians directly under its own control as subjects." Kept apart, forced into peaceful ways, they may be tutored into civilization, first into a pastoral, then into an agricultural state; they must, indeed, be tutored into a sense of private property. For ". . . the insecurity of property, or rather the entire absence of all ideas of property, is the chief cause of their barbarism." Thus "The chain of causes by which the condition of the unhappy race must, if at all, be ameliorated will be this: first, *personal security,* by the entire abolition of war among them, secondly, *permanent habitations,* and thirdly, *notions of property.*"

The hope of civilization is there, albeit dimly, as it was to be with Americans throughout their history. More important, there is a pitying, charitable awareness of the low state of the Indian and the inadequacy of his kind of life in the face of the life of civilized American society. Equally, there is confidence in the manifest destiny of that civilized life. The Indian, if he was to survive, would have to survive not as a savage but as a civilized man. The essence of his savagism was his life as a hunter. This was the master-key to the Indian problem: As hunter he must die; as hunter he was dying. For Hall's, and many another's, hope to civilize the Indian was being dashed by the onrush of civilization itself. And no man could, in the end, regret the onrush of civilization.

A professor of history at the University of Wisconsin-Milwaukee, REGINALD HORSMAN (b. 1931) is an expert on the early national period of the United States. He has written books on the War of 1812 and its causes, but he has devoted his attention as well to Indian affairs—in *Matthew Elliott: British Indian Agent* (1964) and *Expansion and American Indian Policy, 1783–1812* (1967), and in a series of perceptive essays. In the article printed here he argues that American treatment of the Indians was the beginning of a "rationale of expansion" which was readily adapted to an advance over other peoples. Is there a parallel between the early treatment of the Indians and the later doctrine of Manifest Destiny? Can Indian policy help to explain the underlying assumptions of imperialism?*

Reginald Horsman

American Indian Policy and the Origins of Manifest Destiny

The relations of the United States government with the Indian tribes of the American continent have received scant attention from American diplomatic historians. For the most part they have been content to regard this as a domestic concern; an internal problem, sordid but hardly useful for the main course of American foreign policy. There have of course been some exceptions to this pattern, notably in Albert K. Weinberg's study of Manifest Destiny. Yet, although Weinberg's work was written in the 1930's, it has not stimulated diplomatic historians to any determined attempt to analyze in more detail the interconnection of Indian policy and the general ideology of American expansion. In his *Rising American*

Empire Richard Van Alstyne quotes Julius Pratt's statement that "the extension of American rule over the Indian tribes and their lands was imperialism— not recognized as such only because the Indians were so few in number as to be virtually swallowed," but does not develop the point in his own narrative.

The most recent attempt at a general analysis of expansionism is Frederick Merk's *Manifest Destiny and Mission in American History*. In maintaining that peaceful "Mission" not continentalist or imperialist doctrines represented the true national spirit of the United States, Professor Merk dismisses the Indians with a brief reference. He comments of the pre-1840's period that "Regeneration

*Reginald Horsman, "American Indian Policy and the Origins of Manifest Destiny," *University of Birmingham Historical Journal*, XI (1968), 128–140. Reprinted by permission of the University of Birmingham Historical Journal, the copyright holder. Footnotes omitted.

had not been part of the thinking of the American government in dealing with the red man of the wilderness. . . . Numbering but a few hundred thousand in the latitudes of the United States, they were provided for by concentration on reservations. Even Jefferson was content to dispose of them thus."

This slighting of American Indian policy is unfortunate in that it seems clear that American attitudes towards the Indian tell us a great deal about the American attitude to other peoples and about the development of an ideology of expansion. In dealing with the Indians the United States developed a rationale of expansion which was readily adaptable to the needs of an advance over other peoples. Certainly later American expansionists did not view the Indian as a separate concern. By the late nineteenth century the American Indians were viewed as merely one of a number of inferior or degenerate races that had been overwhelmed by the all-conquering Anglo-Saxon. . . .

The initial reaction of the United States to the Indians in the post-1783 period was conditioned by the frontier violence of the Revolutionary years. The Indians had allied with the British in the Revolution, and the impoverished Confederation government at first demanded an eye for an eye; the attacks of the Revolution would be expiated by forced cessions of lands. The Indian resistance to this concept, and the inability of the United States to raise the military force to carry out a blatant policy of conquest, had forced the United States to revert to the colonial policy of purchase by the end of the 1780's. At the same time a new philosophy of Indian relations was coming into being, a philosophy which entwined morality and expansionism.

Since the very beginning of British settlement in North America there had, of course, been elements of moral justification intertwined with warfare, extermination, and the purchase and appropriation of land. It has been said of the early years of settlement that "For giving God and civilization to the Indian, the colonial Englishman was to receive the riches of a new world." The unwillingness of the Indians to give up their own modes of life for those of the newcomers had, however, quickly brought an emphasis on new aspects of morality. If the Indians had ignored God's command to "Be fruitful, and multiply, and replenish the earth, and subdue it," then they would have to make way for those who were quite certain that they were obeying this divine law.

In the late 1780's, and particularly after the formation of the new government in 1789, American leaders began to show a great desire to justify their expansion westwards over the Indians. Their solution to the dilemma of advocating an enlarged area of liberty and the blessings of a free government, while at the same time exterminating the aboriginal inhabitants, was conditioned by the eighteenth-century view of natural man and his improvability. Whatever the attitudes of the frontiersmen, those who formulated American opinion and a national policy in the late eighteenth and the first quarter of the nineteenth century saw the solution to their dilemma in the bringing of civilization to the Indian inhabitants of North America. This attitude was essentially one of great optimism. It did not preach any innate Indian inferiority, but rather viewed the Indian as existing at a lower stage in the evolution of society and civilization. These aboriginal inhabitants were to give up their state of nature, but in exchange were to be given the inestimable blessing of American civilization; the highest and happiest state that man had yet attained.

In adopting the idea that they had a duty of bringing civilization to the Indians, American leaders revealed the extent to which they felt that the eyes of the world were upon them. Henry Knox, Secretary of War under Washington, wrote in 1793 that "If our modes of population and War destroy the tribes the disinterested part of mankind and posterity will be apt to class the effects of our Conduct and that of the Spaniards in Mexico and Peru together. . . ." When he resigned at the end of the following year he showed a sensitivity not only towards contemporary opinion but also to posterity. "A future historian," he wrote, "may mark the causes of this destruction of the human race in sable colors."

From the late 1780's Knox in his public utterances, and in his speeches and letters to the Indians, espoused the idea that the national policy of the United States was to civilize the Indian tribes. This civilization meant, of course, making the Indians into Americans. The ideal was that of an American agrarian society. Ignoring the extensive agricultural development among the Indian tribes with whom the United States was in contact, Knox and the other national leaders of this period placed the whole confrontation in the simple context of a primitive hunting society, on a lower stage of human development. The Indians were to be civilized by the adoption of private property, by the men farming in the American manner, by the women learning to spin and weave, and by the introduction of the rudiments of education and Christianity. Knox asserted in 1792 that the United States wanted the opportunity to impart to the Indians "all the blessings of civilized life, of teaching

you to cultivate the earth, and raise corn; to raise oxen, sheep, and other domestic animals; to build comfortable houses, and to educate your children, so as ever to dwell upon the land."

The full expression of this philosophy of expansion over the Indians came with the Presidency of Thomas Jefferson, who combined a sense of mission to the Indians with a clear vision of the expansionist destiny of the United States. Jefferson was too imbued with eighteenth-century ideas of the natural man to doubt the improvability of the Indian. "I believe the Indian then," he wrote in the 1780's, "to be in body and mind equal to the whiteman." Like Knox, Jefferson ignored the agricultural aspects of Indian society, and preached the adoption of agriculture and private property as the route to the blessings of civilization. "Let me entreat you therefore," he told a delegation of Indians in December 1808, "on the lands now given you to begin every man a farm, let him enclose it, cultivate it, build a warm house on it, and when he dies let it belong to his wife and children after him."

Where Jefferson differed from Knox, and perhaps from most of his contemporaries, was in the enthusiasm with which he espoused the idea of the bringing of civilization, and in the manner in which he took the theory of it to its logical conclusion by arguing for the ultimate assimilation of the Indians within the American population. After telling the Indians to adopt farming and private property, he then argued for the next logical step: "you will unite yourselves with us, and we shall all be Americans. You will mix with us by marriage. Your blood will run in our veins and will spread with us over this great island." In January 1809 Jefferson told another delegation of Indians that "I consider my red children as forming one family with the Whites." Jefferson's Secretary of War, Henry Dearborn, espoused his President's doctrines of the improvability of the Indians. He believed that the progress of civilization among the Indians before 1803 was proof of the practicability of such improvements "as may ultimately destroy all destinctions between what are called Savages and civilized people."

Whatever Jefferson thought of the natural man, however, he was not giving the Indians a choice between their existing state of society and American civilization. Jefferson had no doubt that the United States was offering the Indians the chance of participating in the greatest state of society the world had ever known; a chance to leap over the intervening steps to the high plateau of American civilization. As late as 1824 Jefferson wrote that a traveller coming eastwards from the Rockies to the seaport towns would see the equivalent of a survey in time "of the progress of man from the infancy of creation to the present day." He wrote that living in the first range of mountains in the interior of the country, "I have observed this march of civilization advancing from the seacoast, passing over us like a cloud of light, increasing our knowledge and improving our condition, insomuch as that we are at this time more advanced in civilization here than the seaports were when I was a boy. And where this progress will stop no one can say. Barbarism has, in the meantime, been receding before the steady step of amelioration; and will in time, I trust, disappear from the earth." With this confidence in the ultimate good of what the United States was accomplishing, the Indians could not be allowed to stand in the way. If they did not accept the inestimable benefits of American civilization then they were doomed. In

1812 he commented of Indians who were resisting that "the backward will yield, and be thrown further back. These will relapse into barbarism and misery, lose numbers by war and want, and we shall be obliged to drive them, with the beasts of the forest into the Stony mountains."

The philosophy argued for so eloquently by Jefferson remained the official hope of the United States through to the mid-1820's, and for many individuals persisted even after that date. Madison argued in his inaugural in 1809 that he intended "to carry on the benevolent plans which have been so meritoriously applied to the conversion of our aboriginal neighbors from the degradation and wretchedness of savage life to a participation of the improvements of which the human mind and manners are susceptible in a civilized state." Those who formulated governmental policy continued to argue for assimilation in the following years. In 1816 Secretary of War William Harris Crawford reported to the Senate that it was the desire of the government "to draw its savage neighbors within the pale of civilization." A similar attitude was expressed in 1818 by the chairman of the committee of the House of Representatives on that part of the message of the President regarding Indian affairs. "In the present state of our country, one of two things seems to be necessary," wrote Henry Southard, "either that those sons of the forest should be moralized or exterminated. Humanity would rejoice at the former, but shrink with horror from the latter." Jefferson's ideals were not easily overthrown, for even in the late 1820's James Barbour, Secretary of War under John Quincy Adams, at first hoped that he would be able to incorporate the Indians fully within American society.

The argument that the expansion of

the Americans over the Indians would be a blessing by raising them from a state of savagery to the highest level of civilization thus persisted from the late 1780's to the late 1820's, reaching its high point in the ideas of Thomas Jefferson. What is evident about this phase of American policy is that there was no clear cut separation between the ideals and the sordid reality, no dividing line between an idealistic mission and the realities of expansion. Throughout these years the American frontier pressed relentlessly forward. Knox, Washington, and Jefferson all eagerly sought Indian lands, and in these years the American government used military force, bribery, deception, and every other possible means to expand the arc of American expansion. Jefferson was not only the most earnest in desiring an amalgamation of Americans and Indians, he was also the most realistic in assessing what civilization would mean in terms of acquiring Indian lands. He argued in 1803 that the bringing of civilization to the Indians, with its private property and farming instead of hunting, "will enable them to live on much smaller portions of land." This, argued Jefferson, would produce "a coincidence of interests." While the Indians were learning to live better on less land, an expanding America would require more land. The interrelationship would be for the good of both. These founding fathers had a supreme confidence in the merits of what their government and society had to offer. Its expansion would be for the good of all. If any were so perverse as to refuse what was offered to them then their disappearance in the name of progress was to be regretted but was unavoidable.

In the years between 1815 and 1830 American Indian policy was confronted with a major dilemma, a dilemma which inevitably affected the ideology of expansion. On the one hand confidence in the American mission and progress reached new heights. In the early days of independence there had always been a lingering fear that the experiment of a free, republican government would prove a failure, that those Europeans who prophesied chaos for the American "mobocracy" would prove correct. Yet, in the years after 1815, it was quite clear that the United States was advancing dramatically in total strength. Immigrants were entering American ports in increasing numbers, settlers were pouring west, new states were entering the Union; from one end of the country to the other the story was one of growth and prosperity. Confidence in America as the bastion of freedom and progress reached new heights. In August 1825, American soldier Edmund Pendleton Gaines wrote of the United States as "one great political family, whose fair fame has already attracted the admiration of every civilized country, and whose example has led to the establishment of liberty in South America, and promises to aid in its final extension and permanent establishment throughout every portion of the world." In December 1828 one member of Congress supported the bill for an American establishment on the Columbia River on the grounds that "It proposes an extension of the blessings of civilization, of freedom, and happiness, to the human race."

Yet, while the United States reached new heights of confidence, there seemed little doubt that the dream of Knox and Jefferson was collapsing. In most of the country the Indians were not accepting American civilization, except for its vices. Indian culture had often collapsed, but all too often no coherent pattern had taken its place. Only in the South, among the Cherokees, were American ways winning major victories, and there it was quickly becoming apparent that realities were overwhelming the ideal. At the last instant even privately owned plots of land were wanted by adjacent American settlers. As the United States grew in confidence, as her sense of mission increased, a new rationale had to be found as a basis for Indian relations and expansion. For Knox and Jefferson the Indians had been men in a natural state, capable of improvement, men of equal capabilities in a different stage of society. Yet, as the Indians apparently showed themselves unwilling or incapable of becoming American farmers, and as the United States more than ever became convinced that her expansion benefited the whole world, the feeling that the original inhabitants did not deserve to retain what they possessed became stronger. There had, of course, always been those in the United States who regarded the Indians as mere obstacles to progress, but this view became increasingly powerful in American thinking in the second quarter of the nineteenth century. It ultimately evolved into a philosophy which could justify the appropriation not only of the lands of the Indians but also of those of the Mexicans.

As might be expected, this belief in the ultimate inability of the Indians to be assimilated successfully became most powerful amongst those who had the most interest in acquiring Indian lands, whether held in common or in severalty. Governor George M. Troup of Georgia in 1824 attacked the concept of the amalgamation of the Indians within American society: "The utmost of rights and privileges which public opinion would concede to Indians," wrote Troup, "would fix them in a middle station, between the negro and the white man; and that, as long as they survived this degradation, without the possibility of attaining the

elevation of the latter, they would gradually sink to the condition of the former — a point of degeneracy below which they could not fall; it is likely, before they reached this, their wretchedness would find relief in broken hearts." In the following year Senator Thomas Hart Benton in supporting a road to connect the West with the possessions of Mexico lamented any Indian interference with this object: "Shall a measure of such moment be defeated by a parcel of miserable barbarians, Arabs of the desert, incapable of appreciating our policy, and placing a higher value upon the gun of a murdered hunter, than upon the preservation of all the republics in the world!" This was a long way from Jefferson's concept of the noble savage.

Perhaps the most revealing insight into the new attitude came in a discussion in John Quincy Adams' cabinet in December 1825. This cabinet in many ways well-represented the transformation that was occurring in American thinking. Barbour, the Secretary of War, was still hoping for a solution in Jeffersonian terms, but Secretary of State Henry Clay, who in his public statements often attacked ruthlessness in American expansionism, argued that "it was impossible to civilize Indians; that there never was a full-blooded Indian who took to civilization. It was not in their nature. He believed they were destined to extinction, and, although he would never use or countenance inhumanity towards them, he did not think them, as a race, worth preserving. He considered them as essentially inferior to the Anglo-Saxon race, which were now taking their place on this continent. They were not an improvable breed, and their disappearance from the human family will be no great loss to the world. In point of fact they were rapidly disappearing, and he did not believe that in fifty years from this time there would be any of them left." Adams tells us a good deal about his own opinions as well as those of Barbour by the comment in his diary that "Governor Barbour was somewhat shocked at these opinions, for which I fear there is too much foundation."

The idea that the Indian represented not merely man at a different stage, who could readily be assimilated, but rather an inferior savage who blocked progress gained considerable ground in the late 1820's and 1830's. It seems quite clear that Indian removal must be viewed against this background of disillusionment. Although many men of good will, including Barbour himself, ultimately reached the conclusion that for the good of the Indians, and even to civilize them, they should be removed west of the Mississippi, it is quite clear that many of the politicians who took up the policy of removal had no faith in ultimate civilization. Adams believed that the idea of civilizing the Indians by putting them together in one region west of the Mississippi was impractical, as did several of his cabinet; he was ready to approve the idea because there was nothing better to offer. Removal was a way out of an immediate difficulty; there are few signs that practical politicians really believed those who argued that this was a better way to civilize the Indians.

The basic question for many was that posed by Jackson in his second annual message in December 1830: "What good man would prefer a country covered with forests and ranged by a few thousand savages to our extensive Republic, studded with cities, towns, and prosperous farms, embellished with all the improvements which art can devise or industry execute, occupied by more than 12,000,-000 happy people, and filled with all the blessings of liberty, civilization, and religion?" A member of Congress who supported removal asked "What is history but the obituary of nations?" He wanted to know "are we to check the course of human happiness—obstruct the march of science—stay the works of art, and stop the arm of industry, because they will efface in their progress the wigwam of the red hunter, and put out forever the council fire of his tribe?" There were, of course, still those who believed in the improvability of the Indian, and argued for eventual assimilation, but the prevailing mood and policy of the government had changed. Removal in reality acknowledged the failure of the post-Revolutionary policy of assimilation, and was known to be only a temporary expedient. By 1830 it was quite clear to many Americans that the American population was going to sweep forward to the Pacific.

In the 1830's and 1840's the American view of the Indian merged into a more elaborate ideology which built a basis of justification for American expansion over any lands. The Americans had no need to develop a whole new set of attitudes for they had already been deeply involved in the problem of rationalizing an advance which ruined and dispossessed those with whom they came into contact. More and more the talk was of superior or inferior race rather than of different stages of human society. The idea of the Anglo-Saxons or related races as divinely appointed to civilize the world assumed an increasingly important share of the argument. The confidence in American institutions also reached new heights. "Foreign powers do not seem to appreciate the true character of our Government," Polk announced in his inaugural in 1845. "Our Union is a confederation of independent States, whose policy is peace with each other and all the world. To enlarge its limits is to extend the dominions of peace over additional territories and increasing millions."

Having convinced themselves in the 1820's and 1830's that the failure of the Indians to benefit from the American advance had stemmed from their inherent inferiority, and that Providence had ordained that the Americans would bring peace, freedom, and a better civilization to the world on a stepping-stone of less able races, the proponents of expansionism had no difficulty in extending their arguments to cover the Mexicans. One newspaper made a simple and direct connection: "The Mexicans are *aboriginal Indians*," it was maintained, "and they must share the destiny of their race." Most expansionists were merely content to use analogy. "The Mexican race now see, in the fate of the aborigines of the north, their own inevitable destiny," argued the *Democratic Review*. "They must amalgamate and be lost, in the superior vigor of the Anglo-Saxon race, or they must utterly perish."

The full elaboration of the new notions of race came, however, from Thomas Hart Benton. "I know of no human event, past or present, which promises a greater, and more beneficent change upon earth," argued Benton, "than the arrival of the van of the Caucasian race (the Celtic-Anglo-Saxon division) upon the border of the sea which washes the shore of the eastern Asia. The Mongolian, or Yellow race, is there, four hundred millions in number, spreading almost to Europe; a race once the foremost of the human family in the arts of civilization, but torpid and stationary for thousands of years. It is a race far above the Ethiopian or Black—above the Malay, or Brown, (if we must admit five races)—and above the American Indian, or Red: it is a race

far above all these, but still, far below the White; and, like all the rest, must receive an impression from the superior race whenever they come into contact. It would seem that the White race alone received the divine command, to subdue and replenish the earth! for it is the only race that has obeyed it—the only one that hunts out new and distant lands, and even a New World, to subdue and replenish." With the death of the eighteenth-century Americans the Old Testament was once again gaining ground over the natural law.

In this speech on the future of the American race, Benton talked more specifically of what had happened to the American Indian: "The Red Race has disappeared from the Atlantic coast: the tribes that resisted civilization, met extinction. This is a cause of lamentation with many. For my part, I cannot murmur at what seems to be the effect of divine law. ... Civilization, or extinction, has been the fate of all people who have found themselves in the track of the advancing Whites, and civilization, always the preference of the Whites, has been pressed as an object, while extinction has followed as a consequence of its resistance." This argument that Benton had carried on since the 1820's, that was maintained by Clay, and endorsed by John Quincy Adams and Jackson, formed a consistent thread in the ideology of American expansion. It was still being maintained at the end of the nineteenth century; it was argued with passion that the benefits that American rule conferred, the enlargement of the area of freedom, justified the transformation or dispossession of peoples who might stand in the way. Ultimately, of course, this philosophy depended upon a supreme confidence in the way of life that was being offered, and this confidence was present in abundance. Indians, Mexicans, or Filipinos became merely obstacles in the path to a better world.

In the years from the Revolution to the Mexican War the United States had begun with the presumption that the destruction of the Indians would be a major blot on the national character; a blot for which the United States would have to answer to other nations throughout the world, to future historians, and to God. It can easily be maintained that even in the early years the United States never translated this concern into a practical programme, and that indeed, like Maria Theresa, the more she cried the more she took. Yet, at least in the 1790's and the first decade of the nineteenth century, there was an optimism that all would be well, a belief, however misinformed, that the Indians would assume American civilization, and thus American expansion would directly benefit not only those expanding but also those who stood as a barrier. By the 1820's this concept of Indian improvability was under major attack, and in the 1830's and 1840's a more common assumption was that the Indians had succumbed because they were doomed by Providence, and that the suffering of whoever stood in the way of expansion was nothing beside the benefit to humanity of extending the area of American civilization and freedom. This doctrine was so convenient that it could be used to extend a slave system over a Mexican area that had abandoned slavery.

To treat American Indian policy as a purely domestic concern is to ignore what it tells us of the American attitude towards alien peoples. It would seem fruitful to regard American Indian policy as part of the expansion of Western Europe, particularly the so-called Anglo-Saxons, over peoples throughout the world; an expansion which reached its height at the close of the nineteenth century. In this way American Indian policy can help explain not only the assumptions of what for convenience is called "Manifest Destiny" but also the underlying assumptions of imperialism.

DALE VAN EVERY (b. 1896), a professional writer, in recent years has turned to the history of the American frontier. His four-volume *The Frontier People of America* (1961–1964) chronicles America's march to the West. He followed this work with *Disinherited: The Lost Birthright of the American Indian* (1966), a fascinating story of the removal of the Cherokees. Van Every, though less extreme in his condemnation of the removal than many writers, presents a sad narrative of the uprooting of a noble people. His skillful weaving in of contemporary speeches and reports enables the reader to experience some of the excitement of the time. In the selections given below he describes the actual migration of the Cherokees in 1838 and theorizes about the significance of the event.*

Dale Van Every

Cherokee Removal

History records the sufferings of innumerable peoples whose country was overrun and possessed by alien invaders. There have been relatively fewer recorded occasions, as in the instance of the Babylonian Captivity of the Jews, of an entire people being compelled to abandon their country. This has been universally regarded as the ultimate catastrophe that can befall a people inasmuch as it deprives them of the roots which sustain their identity. Upon the exiles has been pronounced a sentence that by its nature denies all hope of reprieve or relief. To Indians, with their inherited conception of the land of their birth as the repository of those spiritual links to their ancestors which were holy and therefore indissoluble, the prospect of expulsion was clothed with added dreads beyond human evaluation.

The threat was in all its aspects so monstrous that in the spring of 1838 the bewildered masses of the Cherokee people, homeless, hungry, destitute, still remained incredulous that so fearful a fate could actually impend. . . .

Most of the Cherokee to be removed were inhabitants of Georgia and their apprehension was conducted by Georgia militia who had long as a matter of policy been habituated to dealing harshly with Indians. Prison stockades had been erected at assembly and embarkation

*From *Disinherited: The Lost Birthright of the American Indian* by Dale Van Every. Copyright © 1966 by Dale Van Every. Reprinted with omissions by permission of William Morrow and Company, Inc., and Paul R. Reynolds, Inc., 599 Fifth Avenue, New York, N.Y. 10017. Pp. 239, 242–247, 250–251, 255–265. Footnote omitted.

points in which the Cherokee were to be herded and confined while awaiting transportation west. There was little or no likelihood of attempted resistance. Most had been disarmed during Wool's regime and the irresistible military power that had been brought to bear was self-evident. The classic account of what next transpired is that recorded by James Mooney. His contribution to the Bureau of American Ethnology, eventually published in the 19th Annual Report in 1900 under the title *Myths of the Cherokee*, included a history of the Cherokee based upon years of field work. His narrative of the 1838 expulsion was drawn from personal interviews with survivors, white officers as well as Cherokee victims, and had therefore much of the vitality of an eyewitness report:

The history of this Cherokee removal of 1838, as gleaned by the author from the lips of actors in the tragedy, may well exceed in weight of grief and pathos any other passage in American history. Even the much-sung exile of the Acadians falls far behind it in its sum of death and misery. Under Scott's orders the troops were disposed at various points throughout the Cherokee country, where stockade forts were erected for gathering in and holding the Indians preparatory to removal. From these, squads of troops were sent to search out with rifle and bayonet every small cabin hidden away in the coves or by the sides of mountain streams, to seize and bring in as prisoners all the occupants, however or wherever they might be found. Families at dinner were startled by the sudden gleam of bayonets in the doorway and rose up to be driven with blows and oaths along the weary miles of trail that led to the stockade. Men were seized in their fields or going along the road, women were taken from their wheels and children from their play. In many cases, on turning for one last look as they crossed the ridge, they saw their homes in flames, fired by the lawless rabble that followed on the heels of the soldiers to loot and pillage. So keen were these outlaws on the scent that in some instances they were driving off the cattle and other stock of the Indians almost before the soldiers had fairly started their owners in the other direction. Systematic hunts were made by the same men for Indian graves, to rob them of the silver pendants and other valuables deposited with the dead. A Georgia volunteer, afterward a colonel in the Confederate service, said: "I fought through the civil war and have seen men shot to pieces and slaughtered by thousands, but the Cherokee removal was the cruelest work I ever knew." To prevent escape the soldiers had been ordered to approach and surround each house, so far as possible, so as to come upon the occupants without warning. One old patriarch, when thus surprised, calmly called his children and grandchildren around him, and, kneeling down, bid them pray with him in their own language, while the astonished onlookers looked on in silence. Then rising he led the way into exile. A woman, on finding the house surrounded, went to the door and called up the chickens to be fed for the last time, after which, taking her infant on her back and her two other children by the hand, she followed her husband with the soldiers.[1]

Within days nearly 17,000 Cherokee had been crowded into the stockades. Sanitation measures were inadequate in those makeshift concentration camps. Indian families, accustomed to a more spacious and isolated existence, were unable to adapt to the necessities of this mass imprisonment. Hundreds of the inmates sickened. The Indian was by his nature peculiarly susceptible to the depressions produced by confinement. Many lost any will to live and, perceiving no glimmer of hope, resigned themselves to death. Those who had become converts found some comfort in the ministrations of their white and native pastors. In every stockade hymn singings and prayer meetings were almost continuous.

All physical preparations had been

---

[1] Mooney, *Myths of the Cherokee*, p. 130.

carefully planned in advance by the federal authorities in charge of the migration so that little time might be lost in getting the movement under way. In the first and second weeks of June two detachments of some 800 exiles were driven aboard the waiting fleets of steamboats, keelboats and flatboats for the descent of the Tennessee. They passed down the storied waterway by the same route taken by the first white settlers of middle Tennessee under John Donelson in 1780. In the shadow of Lookout Mountain they could survey the wilderness vastnesses from which for 20 years bands of their immediate forebears had sallied to devastate the white frontier, some of them commanded by war chiefs who had lived to be condemned to this exile. Then at Muscle Shoals there came an ironic contrast between the past and the future as Indians being driven from their ancient homeland were committed to transportation by the white man's newest invention. They disembarked from their boats to clamber, momentarily diverted, aboard the cars drawn by the two puffing little locomotives of the railroad recently constructed to move freight and passengers around the rapids. Returning to other boats, they resumed their seemingly interminable journey in the debilitating heat of an increasingly oppressive summer. The attendant army officers, however sympathetic, were helpless against the waves of illnesses. Scott, moving new contingents toward embarkation, was appalled by the reports he received of the mounting death rate among those who had already been dispatched.

The troops assembled for Cherokee expulsion had been by considered governmental design so numerous as to present a show of military power so overwhelming as to provide no faintest invitation to Indian resistance. By the army's first pounce more than nine tenths of the population had been rounded up and driven into the stockades. There remained only a handful of the wilder and more primitive residents of the higher mountains still at large. This handful, however, represented a problem causing Scott serious concern. Were they provoked to resist they might among their remote and cloud-wreathed peaks prove as difficult to apprehend as were the Seminole in their swamps. From this tactical threat sprang the one heroic action to gleam across the otherwise unrelieved despondency of the removal scene.

Tsali was an hitherto undistinguished mountain Cherokee who suddenly soared to an eminence in Cherokee annals comparable to the homage accorded an Attakullaculla, an Old Tassel, a Sequoyah or a John Ross. The stories of his inspired exploit, drawn from eyewitnesses, survivors and references in contemporary official records, vary in detail and have become encrusted by legend but coincide in most essentials. According to the more generally accepted version, a young Cherokee woman upon being assaulted by two soldiers killed both with a hatchet. Tsali hid the weapon under his shirt and assumed responsibility for his kinswoman's act. Scott could not permit the death of his soldiers to remain unpunished and served notice on the band of mountain Cherokee of which Tsali was a member that a scapegoat must be produced. The band felt that it had a reasonable chance to elude pursuit indefinitely but its councils were impressed by the advice of a white trader, William Thomas, a friend of his native customers in the notable tradition of Ludovic Grant, Alexander Cameron and John McDonald. Thomas pointed out the advantage that could be taken of Scott's demand. Tsali was prepared to offer his life for his people. His fellow tribesmen thereupon notified Scott that he would be turned over to American justice in return for American permission to remain unmolested in their mountains. Scott, eager to escape the uncertainties of a guerrilla campaign in so difficult a terrain, agreed to recommend this course to Washington. Tsali was brought in, the voluntary prisoner of his compatriots. His Cherokee custodians were required to serve as the firing squad by which he, his brother and his eldest son were executed. The story became one of the few Indian stories with a happy ending. Thomas continued for years to interest himself in the prolonged negotiations with the governments of the United States and North Carolina which eventually resulted in federal and state recognition of Cherokee title to their mountain holdings. Tsali's sacrifice had permitted this fraction of the nation to become the remnant of the East Cherokee to cling to their homeland where they still are colorful inhabitants of the North Carolina mountains.

Aside from the Tsali episode the round-up of the Cherokee proceeded without interruption. By June 18 General Charles Floyd, commanding the Georgia militia engaged in it, was able to report to his governor that no Cherokee remained on the soil of Georgia except as a prisoner in a stockade. Scott was able to discharge his volunteers June 17 and two days later to dispatch three of his five regular regiments to sectors where military needs were more pressing, two to the Canadian border and one to Florida.

Meanwhile so many migrants were dying in the drought and heat to which the initial removal was subjected that Scott was constrained to lighten the inexorable pressures. The Cherokee Council, which though technically illegal still spoke for the Cherokee people, begged for a postponement to the more healthful weather of autumn. Scott agreed. In July

Ross returned and in conferences with Scott worked out a further agreement under which the Cherokee would cease passive resistance and under his supervision undertake a voluntary migration as soon as weather permitted. Scott was glad to be relieved of further need to use military force. The administration was glad to be offered some defense against the storm of northern criticism. Even Georgia made no serious protest, inasmuch as the Cherokee had already been removed from their land to stockades and there remained no questioning of the state's sovereignty. The one remonstrance, aside from the complaints of contractors, was voiced by the aging Jackson from his retirement at The Hermitage in a letter of August 23, 1838 to Felix Grundy, Attorney General of the United States:

. . . The contract with Ross must be arrested, or you may rely upon it, the expense and other evils will shake the popularity of the administration to its center. What madness and folly to have anything to do with Ross, when the agent was proceeding well with the removal. . . . The time and circumstances under which Gen'l Scott made this contract shows that he is no economist, or is, *sub rosa,* in league with Clay & Co. to bring disgrace on the administration. The evil is done. It behooves Mr. Van Buren to act with energy to throw it off his shoulders. I enclose a letter to you under cover, unsealed, which you may read, seal, and deliver to him, that you may aid him with your views in getting out of this real difficulty.

> Your friend in haste,
> Andrew Jackson

P.S. I am so feeble I can scarcely wield my pen, but friendship dictates it & the subject excites me. Why is it that the scamp Ross is not banished from the notice of the administration?[2]

---

[2] Brown, *Old Frontiers,* p. 512.

Ross, having at last recognized the inevitable, gave to his preparations for the voluntary removal the same driving energy and attention to detail he had until then devoted to resisting removal. All phases of the organization of the national effort were gathered into his hands. All financial arrangements were under his supervision, including the disbursement of the basic federal subsistence allowance of 16 cents a day for each person and 40 cents a day for each horse. For convenience in management en route the 13,000 Cherokee remaining in the stockades were divided into detachments of roughly a thousand to head each of which he appointed a Cherokee commander. At a final meeting of the Cherokee Council it was provided that the constitution and laws of the Nation should be considered equally valid in the west.

The first detachment set out October 1, 1838 on the dreaded journey over the route which in Cherokee memory became known as The Trail of Tears. The last started November 4. The improvement in weather awaited during the tedious summer months in the stockades did not materialize. The spring migration had been cursed by oppressive heat and drought. The fall migration encountered deluges of rain followed by excessive cold. To the hundreds of deaths from heat-induced diseases were now added new hundreds of deaths from prolonged exposure. . . .

The first migrants reached their destination on the plains beyond the western border of Arkansas January 4, 1839. Other contingents continued to straggle in until late in March. Examination of all available records by Grant Foreman, outstanding authority on Indian removal, led him to conclude 4,000 Cherokee had died either during confinement in the stockades or on their 800-mile journey west.

While the Cherokee were traversing their Trail of Tears their fellow southern Indians were committed to afflictions as dismal. The processes of removal were grinding out the cumulative calamities that had been visited upon a race by governmental fiat. . . .

* * *

Removal posed a question of greater concern to humanity than that raised by the immediate sufferings of its victims. No graver charge can be leveled against any government than that it has been proven incapable of dispensing justice. That so serious an indictment could be preferred against the government of the United States clothed the accusation with an added import. Institution of the new American republic upon the principle of devotion to the rights of man had been an event that had encouraged the hopes of mankind everywhere. Its inspired founders had with the most astute forethought fortified democracy by providing balances of power designed to keep government more the servant than the master of the people. Special care had been given to means assuring that the will of the majority must prevail. Yet in the case of Indian removal the application of these carefully instituted processes of democracy had resulted in a flagrant injustice that by flouting their will had bewildered and dismayed the majority of Americans. The miscarriage was made the more startling by the paradoxical circumstance that it sprang not from weaknesses in the American system but from the three primary attributes which were its greatest elements of strength: the division of power between state and national governments, the acceptance of responsibility by political parties and the conception of the country as a haven for refugees from injustice elsewhere.

Of these three elements of strength by far the most dynamic was the reciprocation of authority between state and national governments. At birth the United States had appeared destined to remain a loose confederation of maritime states with a place in the hierarchy of the world's nations on the order of another Holland. It was presumed that eventually white settlement would penetrate the continent's little known interior but that the difficulties imposed upon communication by distance would then lead to the erection of a number of separate nations, a development that did indeed eventuate under comparable circumstances when the peoples of Latin America gained their independence from Spain. The American people were saved from so disastrous a dispersion by the insistence of the first pioneers to cross the mountains that they be assured in their new homes the political privileges they had formerly enjoyed on the seaboard. Their insistence produced the doctrine of the admission to the union of new states each equal in all respects to the original thirteen. The consequences of this counter to the dispersion previously considered inseparable from expansion were prodigious. In 1780 there had been no significant center of American population farther west than a day's journey from waterborne access to the Atlantic and a majority of the Continental Congress had voted to consider the Appalachians the permanent western border of the republic. In 1830, only 50 years later, the dominion of the United States had already been extended to the Rockies. The doctrine of the admission of new and equal states had been the engine that had generated such a growth rate as no other nation had ever experienced. No political device

in the whole history of mankind had ever proved so immediately and overwhelmingly successful.

By its basic tenet, however, it limited the authority of the national government to interfere with the local predilections of the inhabitants of each state. . . .

The national government was, in the actual functioning of the application of political power, precluded from the administration of justice, even in an instance of injustice so flagrant and so widely condemned as that involved in Indian removal.

There could be almost no doubt that a clear majority of the people of the United States disapproved of Indian removal or, at any rate, of the brutal excesses and mortifying breaches of faith that marked the enforcement of the expulsion edict. That local and regional political authority in the south could without serious challenge defy the will of this majority was only in part due to the circumstance that throughout the critical period 1828–36 the President of the United States was the foremost proponent of removal. Congress, presumably more immediately sensitive to the will of the people, grappled again and again with the issue throughout the same period and at every decisive vote evaded giving expression to that will. These equivocal votes in Congress represented responses to the pragmatic functioning of the two party system which in the early 1830's was beginning to coalesce with all the since familiar paraphernalia of national conventions and formulated platforms.

With the emergence of modern democratic governments in the late 18th century it had not been long becoming apparent that no such government could know stability once its electorate had become splintered into a multiplicity of political parties. In the United States, heir to England's political experience, a two party system evolved, after an extemporaneous sequence of experiments and accidents not even distantly contemplated by the framers of the Constitution. By the 1830's the nation's voters had become aligned into two increasingly organized groups, with names still in the process of change, which gave their allegiance either to the party then in control of the government or to the party seeking to seize control at the next election.

The essence of the two party system had by then been discovered to be the necessary preoccupation of each party with the selection of specific means by which it might hold or regain *national* political power. It had been demonstrated to be insufficient to appeal to local or regional sentiments unless such an appeal could be made to fit into a national pattern. Both parties had learned the central lesson that commitment to the election of some of its candidates was not enough. Each had to be committed to lifting a nationwide majority of its candidates into office. As Jackson's second term neared its end the pressures of these party considerations became intense.

It was under such political clouds that the last chance to save the Cherokee from expulsion came with the submission of the New Echota treaty to the Senate for ratification. Less than at any other moment during the Indian removal controversy could there be much doubt of the will of the country's majority. Yet the Senate voted 31 to 15 for ratification. There could be no question, for example, that the consensus in Maine, New Hampshire, New York, Pennsylvania, Indiana and Illinois was opposed to ratification, either out of sympathy for the Indians or of regard for the nation's honor. Yet both senators from every one of these states voted for the treaty. Senators who

voted for it against the sentiments of their constituents, and possibly their own, had a recognized basis upon which to justify their votes. They could argue that victory for their party in the coming election promised to serve the general good of the country far more directly than might any attempt to protect the rights of Indians. The Whig party joined the Democratic party in holding this view, even though there could be no slightest doubt that a vast majority of Whig voters disapproved of removal and even more actively of the treaty. . . .

The American attitude toward justice in relation to minorities had from the outset been anomalous. Through the earlier colonial years the Indians had not been directly involved in this attitude. Instead of having yet become a tension-producing fraction of the white community they had represented a numerous and powerful foreign enemy. The tolerance problem stemmed from the variances in culture between the later arrivals from Europe and Africa and those already established in the colonies. All Americans had originally been the representatives of minority groups, in flight from religious, political or economic disadvantage. All had realized that it was unthinkable to view this new land in any other light than as a haven which must beckon as appealingly to later comers as it had to the first. All had realized that for those who had already arrived their every hope of security and progress depended upon a continuation of the movement as thousands and then hundreds of thousands of other migrants from the old world sought the wider opportunity offered by the new. Yet the later arrivals had seldom been warmly received by their predecessors. In New England the Pilgrims and Puritans had been harshly critical of their later-arriving fellow dis-

sidents. In the Middle Atlantic states a
large proportion of later arrivals had
come under indenture contracts committing them to seven years of bond
service and thereafter to other years of
struggle to outlive the stigma of so hum-
ble an origin. The wave of Scotch-Irish
beginning to arrive in the early 18th
century had been obliged to strain for
a precarious subsistence among the perils
of the most remote frontier. The impulse
to reject had been the more strikingly
evident when the newcomers were of
another nationality. The first groups
of German immigrants were so unfavor-
ably received in New York's Mohawk
Valley that they undertook a second more
desperate migration down the wild Sus-
quehanna River to the Pennsylvania
frontier where they remained for generations a community distinct from their
English neighbors. When the newcomers
were of another race the rejection was
total. The Negroes from Africa, who came
not by choice but compulsion, were committed to slavery. . . .

When he heard of the afflictions to
which the distant Indians were being
subjected the average American was
moved by his normal goodwill to sympathy and indignation. But he was re-
sponding to an idea, not a conviction.
Had he been an inhabitant of an Indian
border area he would have reacted as the
Georgians were reacting. Only in certain
religious and intellectual circles did the
moral response to removal approach an
enduring conviction. It often fell short
even there, as was evidenced by the flare
of active race prejudice ignited among
the God-fearing people of Cornwall by
the Boudinot-Gold marriage. The lesson
had been well read by practical politicians and party managers. It had been
made clear to their shrewd judgment that

it was safe for a congressman or senator
to vote for removal whenever this seemed
a service to the larger aims of his party.
His constituents might compose righteous
memorials and hold mass meetings of
vociferous protest but it was not an issue
on which they were very likely ever to
turn him out of office.

The irreparable injury that had been
inflicted on Indians in the removal period
had been through the instrumentality of
these three principal forces of American
democracy. Personal responsibility for
the application of those forces could be
apportioned among many. President
Jackson could, at the very least, have
softened the impact and ameliorated the
hardship. Instead, for eight years he
devoted the powers of his high office to
initiating and expediting removal, proceeding even to the length of asserting
his interpretation of the Constitution
was invested with a higher authority
than that of the Supreme Court. Immediately responsible for the sufferings
visited upon the Indians was the aggre-
gation of southern politicians, land speculators, contractors, lawyers and wielders
of local police power, acting in concert,
who participated personally in the aggressions and oppressions. Their responsibility was shared by all southerners
who, though many were troubled, looked
the other way and in their zeal to guard
the legitimate principles of states' rights
continued to reelect the officials who
were committing the excesses. A more
shameful responsibility pervaded the
halls of Congress, many of whose members had again and again voted contrary
to their convictions and those of their
constituents. A similar responsibility
lay upon the partisan councils of party
managers who had preferred expediency
to principle. But the primary guilt was

that of the American people. They had not been revolted by the spectacle of injustice. The failure of the government of the United States to dispense justice had not been due to a breakdown of the processes of American democracy. It had been due to the pharisaical unreadiness of the American people to rise to the demands democracy was making upon them.

For this failure a terrible forfeit was to be exacted. The fight for Indian rights had been lost. What had been generally recognized as a great wrong had as generally been determined to be acceptable. A handful of Indians, numbering less than one two-hundredth of the country's population, had been driven into exile. The uncomfortable episode was already fading into the past and, it was hoped, could be forgotten. And so it seemed to be. When in 1840 the Whigs swept the country their triumphant standard bearer was William Henry Harrison who throughout his long career had been as militantly bent upon Indian dispossession as ever had been Andrew Jackson. But an injustice can never be forgotten. The ten-year-long Indian removal controversy had fanned flames that would not subside until they had become a holocaust.

In 1830 there was no threat that sectional differences of opinion regarding slavery might ever irretrievably divide the nation. Slavery had been gradually eliminated in the northern states. The north had found slavery uneconomic and with some moral concern was moved to restrict its spread but so far felt no slightest inclination to attempt to deprive the south of the right to maintain the institution. When the necessity had arisen to deal with slavery in a national sense the counsels of moderate northerners and southerners had prevailed and moderate compromises had been affected. The north was fully as devoted to the principle of the inviolability of private property as was the south. That still rare figure, the abolitionist, was in the 1830's still universally regarded as an un-American anarch to be invariably and justly victimized by street mobs. In no national agency of the government, the Presidency, the Congress, the Supreme Court, or in any northern statehouse, was there in the 1830's any disposition to consider emancipation in any other light than the south's prerogative. Of the awful conflict that was to rend the republic there was as yet no faintest foreshadowing.

It was the eruption of the Indian removal controversy that revealed the latent virulence of sectional antagonism. On this seemingly minor issue the irreconcilability of the two sections' points of view was unmasked in all its spectral dimensions. The issue became a whipping boy upon which each adversary could vent his spleen. The greater issue of slavery had been by mutual consent cloaked in soothing compromise but in the obviously less consequential removal dispute every man could seize the opportunity to gratify his prejudice. Every renewal of debate in congress, every expression of opinion by press or pulpit, became progressively more provocative.

The south might have been content to have successfully defended its stand on states' rights, which it had proved abundantly able to do and which had at no time during the controversy been seriously assailed by the north. It had been the assumption of moral superiority by the north that had aroused the south's full fury. The damage had been done so far as the south was concerned even before the essential faintheartedness of the north's impulse to interfere had been disclosed. It was the north's holier-than-thou attitude that rankled and left the south imbedded for generations in its own special posture of resentful belligerency.

The long controversy had been characterized by an incessant exchange of epithets, threats, aspersions of motive and imputations of dishonor which neither adversary could ever forget or forgive. Had the controversy developed areas of agreement, affording even partial protection for the rights of Indians and some consideration for the views of the north, had there been the same willingness to compromise as in former sectional differences, the passions that had been aroused might have been quieted. But it had burned on through ten agonizing years to a total victory for the south and a total defeat for the north. The south was left with a gnawing sense of secret guilt in having perpetrated so gross an injustice and the north with an equally gnawing and not so secret sense of guilt for having acquiesced in it.

North and south had been maneuvered by the removal issue into the confrontation which they had both previously taken such care to avoid. The heat of the contention had aroused animosities from which there was never to be surcease. The south had been schooled to regard all northerners as sanctimonious hypocrites and the north to regard all southerners as bigoted oppressors of the weak. Each had been provoked to wild threats of subduing the other by arms. North and south had set foot on the road from which there was to be no turning. At the end of that road waited inexorable retribution, the ghastly horrors of the Civil War.

Not all of Helen Hunt Jackson's contemporaries agreed with her views in *A Century of Dishonor*. One who vigorously objected was THEODORE ROOSEVELT (1858–1919), whose solid claims as a historian have been overshadowed by his political preeminence. His *Winning of the West* (1889) contains an appendix in which he listed the good points in America's treatment of the Indians and pointed out the difficult problems that were faced by the government. And in typical forthright fashion he excoriated the "purely sentimental historians" who saw only fraud and injustice.*

Theodore Roosevelt

Foolish Sentimentalists

It is greatly to be wished that some competent person would write a full and true history of our national dealings with the Indians. Undoubtedly the latter have often suffered terrible injustice at our hands. A number of instances, such as the conduct of the Georgians to the Cherokees in the early part of the present century, or the whole treatment of Chief Joseph and his Nez Perçés, might be mentioned, which are indelible blots on our fair fame; and yet, in describing our dealings with the red men as a whole, historians do us much less than justice.

It was wholly impossible to avoid conflicts with the weaker race, unless we were willing to see the American continent fall into the hands of some other strong power; and even had we adopted such a ludicrous policy, the Indians themselves would have made war upon us. It cannot be too often insisted that they did not own the land; or, at least, that their ownership was merely such as that claimed often by our own white hunters. If the Indians really owned Kentucky in 1775, then in 1776 it was the property of Boone and his associates; and to dispossess one party was as great a wrong as to dispossess the other. To recognize the Indian ownership of the limitless prairies and forests of this continent— that is, to consider the dozen squalid savages who hunted at long intervals

*Reprinted by permission of G. P. Putnam's Sons from *The Winning of the West* by Theodore Roosevelt. Copyright 1920 by G. P. Putnam's Sons, Copyright 1948 by G. P. Putnam's Sons, Copyright © 1962 by Harvey Wish. Vol. I, pp. 257–264.

over a territory of a thousand square miles as owning it outright—necessarily implies a similar recognition of the claims of every white hunter, squatter, horse-thief, or wandering cattleman. Take as an example the country round the Little Missouri. When the cattlemen, the first actual settlers, came into this land in 1882, it was already scantily peopled by a few white hunters and trappers. The latter were extremely jealous of intrusion; they had held their own in spite of the Indians, and, like the Indians, the inrush of settlers and the consequent destruction of the game meant their own undoing; also, again like the Indians, they felt that their having hunted over the soil gave them a vague prescriptive right to its sole occupation, and they did their best to keep actual settlers out. In some cases, to avoid difficulty, their nominal claims were bought up; generally, and rightly, they were disregarded. Yet they certainly had as good a right to the Little Missouri country as the Sioux have to most of the land on their present reservations. In fact, the mere statement of the case is sufficient to show the absurdity of asserting that the land really belonged to the Indians. The different tribes have always been utterly unable to define their own boundaries. Thus the Delawares and Wyandots, in 1785, though entirely separate nations, claimed and, in a certain sense, occupied almost exactly the same territory.

Moreover, it was wholly impossible for our policy to be always consistent. Nowadays we undoubtedly ought to break up the great Indian reservations, disregard the tribal governments, allot the land in severalty (with, however, only a limited power of alienation), and treat the Indians as we do other citizens, with certain exceptions, for their sakes as well as ours. But this policy, which it would

be wise to follow now, would have been wholly impracticable a century since. Our central government was then too weak either effectively to control its own members or adequately to punish aggressions made upon them; and even if it had been strong, it would probably have proved impossible to keep entire order over such a vast, sparsely peopled frontier, with such turbulent elements on both sides. The Indians could not be treated as individuals at that time. There was no possible alternative, therefore, to treating their tribes as nations, exactly as the French and English had done before us. Our difficulties were partly inherited from these, our predecessors, were partly caused by our own misdeeds, but were mainly the inevitable result of the conditions under which the problem had to be solved; no human wisdom or virtue could have worked out a peaceable solution. As a nation, our Indian policy is to be blamed, because of the weakness it displayed, because of its short-sightedness, and its occasional leaning to the policy of the sentimental humanitarians; and we have often promised what was impossible to perform; but there has been little wilful wrong-doing. Our government almost always tried to act fairly by the tribes; the governmental agents (some of whom have been dishonest, and others foolish, but who, as a class, have been greatly traduced), in their reports, are far more apt to be unjust to the whites than to the reds; and the Federal authorities, though unable to prevent much of the injustice, still did check and control the white borderers very much more effectually than the Indian sachems and war chiefs controlled their young braves. The tribes were warlike and bloodthirsty, jealous of each other and of the whites; they claimed the land for their hunting-grounds, but their claims all conflicted with one another; their knowledge of their own boundaries was so indefinite that they were always willing, for inadequate compensation, to sell land to which they had merely the vaguest title; and yet, when once they had received the goods, were generally reluctant to make over even what they could; they coveted the goods and scalps of the whites, and the young warriors were always on the alert to commit outrages when they could do it with impunity. On the other hand, the evil-disposed whites regarded the Indians as fair game for robbery and violence of any kind; and the far larger number of well-disposed men, who would not willingly wrong any Indian, were themselves maddened by the memories of hideous injuries received. They bitterly resented the action of the government, which, in their eyes, failed to properly protect them and yet sought to keep them out of waste, uncultivated lands which they did not regard as being any more the property of the Indians than of their own hunters. With the best intentions, it was wholly impossible for any government to evolve order out of such a chaos without resort to the ultimate arbitrator—the sword.

The purely sentimental historians take no account of the difficulties under which we labored nor of the countless wrongs and provocations we endured, while grossly magnifying the already lamentably large number of injuries for which we really deserve to be held responsible. To get a fair idea of the Indians of the present day, and of our dealings with them, we have fortunately one or two excellent books, notably *Hunting Grounds of the Great West* and *Our Wild Indians,* by Colonel Richard I. Dodge (Hartford, 1882); and *Massacres of the Mountains,* by J. P. Dunn (New York, 1886). As types of the opposite class, which are worse than

valueless, and which nevertheless might cause some hasty future historian, unacquainted with the facts, to fall into grievous error, I may mention *A Century of Dishonor,* by H. H. (Mrs. Helen Hunt Jackson), and *Our Indian Wards* (George W. Manypenny). The latter is a mere spiteful diatribe against various army officers, and neither its manner nor its matter warrants more than an allusion. Mrs. Jackson's book is capable of doing more harm because it is written in good English, and because the author, who had lived a pure and noble life, was intensely in earnest in what she wrote, and had the most praiseworthy purpose—to prevent our committing any more injustice to the Indians. This was all most proper; every good man or woman should do whatever is possible to make the government treat the Indians of the present time in the fairest and most generous spirit, and to provide against any repetition of such outrages as were inflicted upon the Nez Percés and upon part of the Cheyennes, or the wrongs with which the civilized nations of the Indian Territory are sometimes threatened. The purpose of the book is excellent, but the spirit in which it is written cannot be called even technically honest. As a polemic, it is possible that it did not do harm (though the effect of even a polemic is marred by hysterical indifference to facts). As a history it would be beneath criticism, were it not that the high character of the author and her excellent literary work in other directions have given it a fictitious value and made it much quoted by the large class of amiable but maudlin fanatics concerning whom it may be said that the excellence of their intentions but indifferently atones for the invariable folly and ill effect of their actions. It is not too much to say that the book is thoroughly untrustworthy from cover to cover, and that not a single statement it contains should be accepted without independent proof; for even those that are not absolutely false are often as bad on account of so much of the truth having been suppressed. One effect of this is, of course, that the author's recitals of the many real wrongs of Indian tribes utterly fail to impress us, because she lays quite as much stress on those that are non-existent, and on the equally numerous cases where the wrongdoing was wholly the other way. To get an idea of the value of the work, it is only necessary to compare her statements about almost any tribe with the real facts, choosing at random; for instance, compare her accounts of the Sioux and the plains tribes generally with those given by Colonel Dodge in his two books; or her recital of the Sandy Creek massacre with the facts as stated by Mr. Dunn—who is apt, if anything, to lean to the Indian's side.

These foolish sentimentalists not only write foul slanders about their own countrymen, but are themselves the worst possible advisers on any point touching Indian management. They would do well to heed General Sheridan's bitter words, written when many Easterners were clamoring against the army authorities because they took partial vengeance for a series of brutal outrages: "I do not know how far these humanitarians should be excused on account of their ignorance; but surely it is the only excuse that can give a shadow of justification for aiding and abetting such horrid crimes."

ALDEN T. VAUGHAN (b. 1929), professor of history at Columbia University, has shaken the accepted view of Puritan harshness toward the Indians in his book *New England Frontier: Puritans and Indians, 1620–1675* (1965). Examining the relations with the Indians in New England in the period before King Philip's War, he discovers that the old position cannot be accepted. In the selection from his "Epilogue and Conclusion" printed below he strikes at six myths with which he disagrees. "The root of the misunderstanding . . . ," he says, "may lie in a failure to recognize the nature of the two societies that met in seventeenth century New England." Does the limited period he studies weaken general conclusions about colonial treatment of the Indians that might be drawn from his book?*

Alden T. Vaughan

Puritans and Indians

Almost one hundred years ago the eminent New England historian John Gorham Palfrey prefaced his chapters on King Philip's War with a brief evaluation of Indian-white relations up to that event. Much that Palfrey wrote is open to criticism: his undisguised contempt for Indian intelligence and character, his unmistakable Protestant bias, his unabashed filiopiety. But at least the clergyman-historian was unencumbered by the myriad myths that have grown up since his time to cloud our understanding of the Puritans and their treatment of the New England Indians. Not all historians since the mid-nineteenth century have fallen prey to these myths—Herbert L. Osgood and Charles M. Andrews were too

well grounded in primary sources to succumb at all—but the majority of writers have tended to ascribe the "typical" frontier pattern to one area of the country where it does not apply, or to ascribe to the New England Puritans certain attitudes and characteristics that they simply did not possess.

The sources of the misconceptions are difficult to trace. The writings of Helen Hunt Jackson, the frontier thesis of Frederick Jackson Turner, and only recently the sharp reaction in America against racial intolerance probably have all had a share in creating a number of assumptions that may be valid for other places and other times but have little application to the New England frontier before

*From *New England Frontier: Puritans and Indians, 1620–1675* by Alden T. Vaughan, by permission of Little, Brown and Co. Copyright © 1965 by Alden T. Vaughan. Pp. 322–333, 336–338. Footnotes omitted.

King Philip's War. Similarly, it is through innumerable writers that we have inherited those notions about "Puritanism" which Samuel Eliot Morison, Perry Miller, Edmund Morgan and others have labored so hard to dispel. Still myths die hard, and once established, the patterns and prejudices quickly descend from historian to popularizer and from popularizer to the general public. In any event, the traditional approaches to the story of the Puritan and the American Indian have been characterized more by hindsight than by insight.

The root of the misunderstanding—for both the historian and the layman—may lie in a failure to recognize the nature of the two societies that met in seventeenth century New England. One was unified, visionary, disciplined, and dynamic. The other was divided, self-satisfied, undisciplined, and static. It would be unreasonable to expect that such societies could live side by side indefinitely with no penetration of the more fragmented and passive by the more consolidated and active. What resulted, then, was not—as many have held—a clash of dissimilar ways of life, but rather the expansion of one into the areas in which the other was lacking. Thus Puritan law and order did not contest with Indian law and order; the latter was amorphous and variable, and the extension of the colonists' system of jurisprudence met with far more encouragement than resistance from the natives. So too, the Indians eagerly sought involvement in the Puritans' economic system. In short, the native society—or more properly societies, for there were several—actively drew Puritan civilization into its own primitive environment. The important question is therefore not whether the Puritans should have expanded, but how well and moderately and justly they carried out the expansion

of their brand of western civilization into the neolithic world of the American Indian.

Even without a disparity of cultures, Puritan and Indian might have found ground for animosity in concepts of racial purity or racial superiority, had either held such notions. Some historians have wrenched Puritan rhetoric out of its context and given it a racist meaning that was never there. Other historians have waxed loquacious over the Indians' "pride of race"—a conception unknown to the natives of seventeenth century New England. And implicit in the historian's argument that the natives defeated themselves in the long run by their inability to join together against the white man is a belief that they *should* have acted together as a race. To argue in this fashion is to be far more race-minded than Puritans or Indians ever were. They, unlike many of their descendants, saw that considerations of justice, religion, humanity, political policy, economic well-being, or even that strange intangible called "progress" were more valid reasons for determining actions and allegiances than the chance assignment to a particular ethnic category.

The whole matter of Indian participation in the wars of seventeenth century New England is a case in point. From Massasoit's revelation of Corbitant's scheme against the Pilgrims in 1621, to the reports of Ninigret's conspiracies in the forties and fifties, to the dramatic disclosures made on the eve of King Philip's War, it was the red man who warned his white neighbor of impending attack. When war did come, the Indians played a still more conspicuous role as allies to the settlers. The reader will recall the contributions made by the native confederates of the Puritans to the outcome of the Pequot conflict and King Philip's

War. After Mason's opening victory against the Pequots at Mystic—where he was aided by Mohegans, Narragansetts, and Eastern Niantics—the surviving enemies had been prey to almost every tribe in New England; and in the struggle with Philip, the colonial ranks were swelled by native cohorts. In both wars the assistance of friendly Indians as scouts and guides, while less dramatic, was perhaps equally important to the cause of the settlers: witness for example the contribution of Wequash in leading Mason's army undetected to Mystic Fort. Finally, it should not be forgotten that the three men who posed the greatest challenge to Puritan security in the seventeenth century were slain by fellow Indians: Sassacus by the Mohawks, Miantonomo by Uncas, and Philip by one of his former subjects.

In peacetime as in war, many of the natives of New England identified their interests and loyalties with those of the colonists. Ever since Squanto attached himself to the Pilgrim Fathers, a significant number of Indians chose to cast their lot, in part at least, with the white man's society. The manner and degree varied. Large numbers of natives came no closer than to mesh their economic habits with the more prosperous economy of the Puritans, or to make use of some of the tools, trinkets, or garments of the English. Others looked to the colonies for military protection or for arbitration in native disputes. The praying Indians went still further toward assimilation in the Puritan culture and accepted its deepest religious convictions. Finally, a few natives tried to merge their lives completely with colonial society by joining its communities and adopting all its customs and values.

In choosing to live partly or wholly in the white man's way, the American In-dian was being neither weak nor disloyal to his own heritage. There is no reason to expect the member of a primitive society to forego the alluring offerings of a wealthier and more sophisticated civilization. To be on the side of "progress" is not necessarily to be right; to resist "progress," on the other hand, is not necessarily noble. While there is a fascination in studying primitive cultures, there is no reason to expect the participants in those cultures to remain stagnant in the face of better alternatives. No society of any appreciable magnitude has ever chosen to reject "westernization," nor has western civilization itself remained static. Adaptation, amalgamation, and integration have been the hallmarks of human progress, not only in the material realm but in human rights and social justice. There is no reason why the Indians of New England should not have shared in this almost universal trend if they so chose. There is some evidence that a far greater number of them would have thrown off the shackles of the Stone Age if their sachems had not been so reluctant to jeopardize their own power and wealth.

The tragedy is that in the long run the red man of New England succeeded neither in amalgamation nor in resistance. Rather, by 1750 the Indian had almost disappeared from the New England scene. There is therefore a temptation to suspect that Puritan policy subtly aimed at exterminating or utterly subduing the native. But here again, the myth is easier to repeat than to support. The fact that one ethnic group deteriorated while another flourished in a given area is not proof of a causal relationship. The rise of the white man and the subsequent decline of the red man are unquestionably interrelated, but only in rather subtle and unconscious ways. Perhaps the best way of understanding the interplay of forces is to restate some of the things that the New Englander did *not* do to the native.

(1) The Puritan did not push the New England Indian off his land. The myth of the early colonist as a land-grabber is one of the most persistent, for on the surface it has an immediate aura of validity. The red man once owned all the land, now he owns little or none: hence, the Puritan must have tricked, cajoled, or forced the Indian out of his birthright.

But does this *prima facie* evidence accord with the ascertainable facts? The Indian did not hold that the entire continent belonged to him; it was rather the white man who introduced the idea that it was a red man's continent that purchase alone could transform into the domain of the white. The Indian only knew that he had enough land for himself and his tribe; the remainder was as truly *vacuum domicilium* to him as it was to the Puritan. The native therefore did not object to the occupation of proximate territory by European settlers, so long as the immigrants came as friends rather than foes. Hence the Wampanoags did not contest Pilgrim settlement at Plymouth and the Massachusetts did not object to the establishment of English towns around Boston Harbor. If the white man should desire indisputable possession of territory over which some tribe had an ancient claim, the sachems were ever ready to relinquish their title for a payment—a payment that sometimes appeared modest in European eyes, but that always accorded with the values of Algonquian society. Deeds were carefully drawn, signed only after translation by a competent interpreter (as often as not an Indian), and filed with responsible colonial officials.

(2) The Puritan did *not* deplete the food sources of the natives. The supply of meat unquestionably diminished as an increasing English population raised the demand while it reduced the forest areas. But it had not been on game that the Indian subsisted, but upon vegetable and grain crops, only supplemented by seafood and meat. There is simply no evidence, and even less logic, to support a charge that the seventeenth century Puritan colonists deprived the red man of a food supply, on which, in fact, the Indian had not been dependent in the first place.

(3) The Puritan did *not* upset the Indian's economic pattern by underpaying him for goods and services. The Indian parted with two major trade commodities: fur and land. Fur, an item he had never considered of great marketable value, suddenly came into demand with the arrival of the settlers, thus bringing a new source of wealth to the Indian. His new prosperity, in turn, permitted him to obtain items—both native and imported—which he desired.

The sale of land, of course, imposed no hardship on a people who subsisted primarily on agricultural crops. The area actually devoted to gardens was an infinitesimal fraction of the New England soil. Most of the rest—excepting village sites, favorite fishing and trapping areas, and the like—was surplus land to the Indians. In 1620 there were more than four square miles of land for every Indian man, woman, and child in New England. It is not surprising, therefore, that the natives were glad to sell some of it to the newcomers. Moreover, the deeds of sale clearly indicate that the native usually retained the right to hunt and fish; sometimes he even retained the right to cultivate crops, though this occurred less frequently because the Indian rarely parted with cultivated land. Finally, the Puritan colonies followed the English custom of allowing the public to hunt and fish on unfenced land.

And what was the Indian receiving in

exchange for his land and his furs? A familiar theme in American historical literature has the white trader enticing the Indian out of his magnificent forest heritage with a glitter of glass beads and a splash of pretty colored cloth—or far worse, a whiff of strong waters. Trinkets, of course, were often exchanged, and to the real satisfaction of their new native possessors; very real also was the liquor trade. But the inventories of New England merchants and traders reveal a steady flow of solid goods into the Indian economy—of new tools and materials far superior to anything the Algonquian had known, and wampum that served as currency for whites as well as Indians. (The increase in the value of wampum stands, in itself, as an example of the invigorating effect upon the native economy of English settlement.) That the white man, particularly in the twentieth century, should think hoes, hatchets, and cloth less valuable than land does not alter the fact that the seventeenth century Indian believed he was getting a bargain. And it could easily be argued that the red man's sense of values in cherishing functional tools and textiles was more commendable than the white man's craving for beaver skins that served no better purpose than to adorn the top of his head. In any event, the fact of frequent and voluntary sale is conclusive evidence that neither side thought it was being cheated. It is a peculiar theory of economic morality that judges the equity of a barter by the value of the commodities three centuries later.

(4) The Puritan did *not* kill off the Indians in a series of protracted military actions. True, the Pequot tribe sustained heavy losses in 1637; the Wampanoags, Narragansetts, Nipmucs, and Pocumtucks suffered similarly in 1676. Yet total casualties of the two "Indian wars" account for at most fifteen or twenty per cent of the decline in native population. And, as has been noted above, so many of the natives fought on the English side in both wars that neither struggle can be described accurately as Puritan wars against the Indians. What casualties the Puritan inflicted on some of the Indians of New England, he inflicted with the aid and encouragement of an equal number of others. Statistical accuracy is impossible in such a matter, but it is not unlikely that Puritan militia killed fewer natives in the years 1620–1676 than did their red allies. It is also important to remember that intertribal rivalries played a major role in bringing on the wars. John Oldham was killed by Narragansett subjects, probably for trading with the Pequots; Cutshamekin of the Massachusetts tribe may have fired the first fatal shot of the Pequot War; while the River tribes, Narragansetts, and Mohegans all were eager for revenge on Sassacus's tribe. King Philip's War was less related to intertribal rivalry, but it is perhaps significant that it was sparked by the assassination of one Indian by several others, presumably under Philip's direction.

(5) The Puritan did *not* drive the Indian to despair through repeated injustices and cruelties. Certainly, colonial laws were framed by Puritans on Puritan premises, and of course were in large part determined by intelligent self-interest. Examples include colonial and intercolonial regulations against war; prohibition of the sale of firearms, other weapons, and liquor to Indians; and temporary wartime restrictions on the travel of unaccompanied natives into areas settled by colonists. But such rules were intended for the safety of all, and they seem to have had the general endorsement of native leaders. The prohibition against war, for example, was favored by

all except those who, at any given moment, desired to wage war.

Most New England Indians, however, were rarely affected by the Puritan legal machinery unless they voluntarily submitted to it. When whole tribes, through their sachems, agreed by written treaty to obey the government and laws of a particular colony, or when an individual native signified his desire to join white society, they became citizens of the colony in almost the same sense that white settlers were citizens. They obeyed the law or paid the prescribed penalty. The subject Indian was treated differently, to be sure, in that he was occasionally the object of such special legislation as exemption from military service or the restrictions imposed on the praying Indians during Philip's War. Under certain circumstances, then, he was the victim of discrimination. But for the seventeenth century, these were unusually mild proscriptions on a people that was not only an ethnic minority but a religious and political minority as well. And in each instance of discriminatory legislation, the motive was security, not social or religious bias.

Many tribes had little contact with colonial laws, encountering only those passed by the Confederation of New England or by the individual colonies for insuring the public peace. Occasionally an individual native from an autonomous tribe would become involved as plaintiff, defendant, or witness in litigation resulting from assault, trespass, or some other crime. To the extent that he rarely saw Indians on the jury, he was deprived of equal treatment before the law. But problems of language and learning made the native an unlikely jury prospect, although three of the Puritan colonies did at times seat Indian jurors in cases in which both principals were Indians.

When the Indian came to the Puritans' courts for civil or criminal cases, he could expect just treatment. It would be a mistake to gauge the fairness of the Puritan legal system on the basis of whether it distributed favorable verdicts in equal numbers to red men and white. A host of variants might create an understandable numerical imbalance. Indians, for example, owned far less personal property than English settlers, and it is not surprising that when an Indian and an Englishman were pitted against each other in cases of theft, the Indian was usually the defendant and more often than not was found guilty. On the other hand, since the natives owned far fewer cattle and swine than the whites, it was usually the native who was plaintiff and won the verdict in charges concerning the destruction of property by livestock. Case by case, the New England court records reveal no apparent discrimination against the Indian. A white plaintiff was not assured of a favorable decision, nor an Indian plaintiff of an adverse one.

Certainly in respect to punishments the Indian was not treated more harshly than the colonist. Murder of a white by an Indian merited the death penalty, and so did the reverse. For other crimes the Indian was punished in the customary ways: stocks, whipping, fines, imprisonment; and there is no evidence that such penalties were inflicted with greater harshness or magnitude on the Indian than on his white neighbor. That Indian prisoners of war were sometimes enslaved is by modern standards the blackest of marks against Puritan society, and it is slight mitigation that this was a common custom in the seventeenth century— among red men and whites alike. It is equally distressing that Puritan courts occasionally sold captives and debtors to the West Indies. Still, it is of some significance, though small consolation, that this was usually a military safeguard rather than a judicial sentence, and that the few who were sold out of the colonies during peacetime were victims of the Puritan search for a punishment comparable to banishment that could be applied to a chronic transgressor. It is significant too that war captives and prisoners sold for default of debts who were kept as slaves within New England were treated as indentured servants, and most of them probably did not serve more than a few years.

(6) Finally, the Puritan was *not* indifferent to the physical, moral, and spiritual well-being of the natives. He sincerely endeavored to convince the red man of the benefits of civilized society and of the religion that to the Puritan represented consolation in this life and salvation in the next. The Puritan never forced his views on the natives, nor did his missionaries ever relent in their efforts to persuade.

Closely allied to the Puritan's attempts to spread Christianity were his attempts to spread education. The creation of schools in the praying towns, the opening of village common and grammar schools to Indian youths, and the establishment of an Indian College at Harvard stand as eloquent testimony to the sincerity of the Puritan educational effort.

Finally, Edward Winslow's medical ministrations to Massasoit and his people in the 1620's and the many kindnesses shown by the Bay Colony settlers to sufferers in the plague of the early thirties are but two of the many evidences that the Puritan's humanitarian interest in his red neighbor's welfare took individual as well as institutional forms. . . .

* * *

It was not through threat of starvation, or demon rum, or the greed and malice of white settlers that so many of the Indians were eliminated from New England, but through three agencies: disease, war, and migration. Most important, probably, was disease, for from the first coming of the white man the Indian was exposed to a number of new sicknesses to which he was highly susceptible. Even before the Pilgrims arrived, disease had swept away one-third or more of the native population. Subsequent epidemics reduced it still further. The new maladies struck down friend and foe alike; if anything they showed a perverse preference for the native who had taken up the white man's ways. For example, Squanto died less than two years after adhering to the Plymouth settlers, Indian students in English schools rarely lasted much longer, and the praying Indians suffered heavily too. On the other hand, those Indians who were partially or wholly segregated from the white man did not incur as high mortality rates as did those who mingled more directly with colonial society. It is ironic that the Puritans of New England, innocent of so many of the charges against them, should unwittingly cause the devastation of their Indian neighbors through communicable disease.

Of war, enough has already been said to make it clear that armed conflicts resulted in heavy casualties but were certainly not solely responsible for the sharp decline in Indian population. Nor were they ever simple clashes of white man against red. On the other hand, since warfare ordinarily takes the lives of young men, and since intertribal warfare continued to add its toll to the list of victims, the final effect of seventeenth century conflict was a serious check on the native population. These wars, of course, continued into the eighteenth century, and helped to maintain the steady decline of native population after 1675.

Finally, many Indians from fear of diseases, from wartime necessity, or from a desire to escape the challenge of the new era, moved west and north to areas still untouched by the European. But others remained behind to meet the spreading influence of the more advanced society. Much like the white frontiersmen of the eighteenth and nineteenth centuries, the New England Indian responded in a variety of ways to the advance of civilization into his area. Some, especially the tribal leaders who had enjoyed great power under the old regime, resisted the new ways. Others eagerly took them up, while still others remained where they were born and quietly ignored all innovation.

* * *

From the perspective of the 1960's, it is easy to detect sins of omission in the Puritan's conduct of Indian affairs, and there is much we can point to that he did with less tact and judgment than a later generation could desire. But at the same time, it is hard to chastise the Puritans for failing to do better a job that their contemporaries did not perform as well. The record of the New England colonies, when tested comparatively rather than absolutely, becomes another credit on their list of achievements in the New World. The suspicion and hostility of the pre-Pilgrim period was changed during the early decades of Puritan settlement into an atmosphere of amity and cooperation, and that atmosphere remained prevalent until 1675. There were exceptions, of course. It would have been too much to expect any two large groups of seventeenth century mortals to live in such proximity without occasional friction. The Indian tribes had not been able to live together peaceably before the European came, the European nations could not live together peaceably on either side of the Atlantic, and even within the Puritan colonies there was something less than complete tranquillity. This made it unlikely that natives and New Englanders, separated by vast differences in political, economic, religious, and social patterns, could share the same corner of the continent without occasional clashes of interests and arms. But what is most significant is that when troubled times came, the division of forces was not along purely ethnic lines. Red man and white had enough in common to pick their quarrels over issues rather than over skin color. This, in itself, is a sign that the New England Puritans had treated the Indians not as a race apart, but as fellow sinners in God's great universe. It also makes more poignant the ultimate failure of the Puritans' mission to the wilderness.

A fresh, unstereotyped view of early Indian policy is provided by BERNARD W. SHEEHAN (b. 1934), recently a fellow at the Institute for Early American History and Culture at Williamsburg and now a member of the history department at Indiana University. In the article reprinted here he reviews the writings of historians on Indian relations and offers trenchant criticism of their work. The article is an extremely valuable bibliographical essay, and the full footnotes have therefore been retained. It is in addition a forceful expression of Sheehan's own views, which contrast markedly with the traditionally harsh criticisms of Anglo-American dealings with the Indians. What new dimensions does Sheehan add to the study of the problem of Indian-white relations?*

Bernard W. Sheehan

Indian-White Relations in Early America

The white man is guilty. He has been charged with the destruction of the American Indian, the evidence has been presented, and the verdict returned for all to see. The sorry remnants of the American aborigine in our own day, beneficiaries and victims of the government's largess, testify to the overwhelming culpability of the civilized intruder in the Indian's domain. No doubt the objective fact is true: the modern Indian does, at least in the white man's mind, present a depressing contrast to his past eminence; and the occupation of the American continent by the European settler is surely the cause of his decline. The story has been recounted often enough to be part of the American folklore. Whether the set-

tler out of sheer viciousness or unconquerable greed drove the native population from its ancestral home, decimating tribe after tribe until the pathetic survivors were herded on to reservations in the late nineteenth century, or merely brought to the new land the trappings of a foreign environment, liquor and disease, hostile to the Indian's continued existence, the result was the same. And the criminal was still the civilized European.

The archetypal historical definition of the white man's guilt was presented in 1881 by Helen Hunt Jackson in her *Century of Dishonor*. Though frankly polemical (the cover of the second edition in 1886 was stamped in red with a quotation

*Bernard W. Sheehan, "Indian-White Relations in Early America: A Review Essay," *William and Mary Quarterly,* 3rd ser., XXVI (April, 1969), 267–286.

from Benjamin Franklin: "Look upon
your hands! They are stained with the
blood of your relations."), the volume
also made historical pretensions. But
more important, it revealed the deep
sense of guilt many white men felt at
the fate of the Indian, and it contrived
to formulate a scheme that would portray
the native as a hapless victim and the
white man as a merciless aggressor. In
tone sentimental, it was in substance a
moral tract whose purpose was to convict
civilization of its crimes against the aborigine; and history was subordinate to
this greater object.

Besides the melodrama of murder,
robbery, cruelty, perfidy, and the white
man's generally outrageous behavior,
the burden of Mrs. Jackson's book conveyed a basic interpretation of Indian-
white relations. In the first pages she
spelled out her conviction that the Indians were organized into sovereign nations
and that the whites were obliged under
international law to treat them as such.
The natives had a right to the soil that
should have been honored and their
agreements carried the force of sovereign
contracts. In repeatedly violating treaties,
the whites had set themselves outside the
law and were thereby subject to arbitrary
punishment by any civilized nation that
should see fit to call them to account.[1]
Indian negotiators behaved not in the
manner of "ignorant barbarians" but as
"clear-headed, statesman-like rulers, in-
sisting on the rights of their nation."[2] The
whites, especially on the frontier, were
largely responsible for the violence that
repeatedly flared between the two societies. And the conflict was not merely
the fortuitous meeting of two groups of

people with different interests. On the
white man's side there was a measure of
calculation. "Thus early in our history
was the ingenious plan evolved of first
maddening the Indians into war, and then
falling upon them with exterminating
punishment." Indian violence was the
exception in the sum of frontier conflict
and then it was either in response to the
white man's aggression or instigated by
the white for his own interest.[3] The Indian was depicted as the innocent victim
of a hostile and unprincipled civilization
and, adding pathos to his decline, as the
possessor of a public order and private
virtues not dissimilar to those supposedly
characteristic of civilization.

To be sure, later historians, though
deeply sympathetic to the Indian's cause,
were neither so sentimental nor so one-
sided in their treatment of Indian-white
relations. Yet the Indian seemed consis-
tently to manifest the qualities of national
independence and most poignantly to
suffer from the crass aggressiveness of the
whites. For example, in her treatment of
Indian removal, the culminating event of
Indian-white relations in the early period,
Annie H. Abel described with admirable
detachment the process through which the
Indians were induced to move west of the
Mississippi.[4] Throughout the Indians
performed as any other sovereign people,
carrying on long and difficult negotiations with a power of equal independence.
The other segment of the story was told by
Grant Foreman in two studies, both dwell-
ing on the actual process of removal.[5]

[1] Helen Hunt Jackson, *A Century of Dishonor: A Sketch of the United States Government's Dealings with Some of the Indian Tribes,* 2d ed. (Boston, 1886), 29.
[2] *Ibid.,* 41.
[3] *Ibid.,* 33–34, 40, 339, 405–406.
[4] Annie H. Abel, "The History of Events Resulting in Indian Consolidation West of the Mississippi River," American Historical Association, *Annual Report for the Year 1906* (Washington, 1908), I, 233–450.
[5] Grant Foreman, *Indian Removal: The Emigration of the Five Civilized Tribes of Indians,* new ed. (Norman [orig. pub., Norman, 1932], 1953); and Grant Foreman, *The Last Trek of the Indians* (Chicago, 1946).

Here the Indians "with bitter sorrow in their hearts, weakened by hardship and privation, decimated by disease, oppressed by penury, despondent and disheartened," struggled over their "trail of tears" to exile in the west.[6] In Annie Abel's account the native was scarcely recognizable as an Indian and in Foreman's two volumes, though solid and moderate works, the victimized aborigine could not but cast his shadow on the overwhelming guilt of the white man.

The white man's crime, however, was not an abrupt or even readily definable act. After all, whatever the Indian suffered as a consequence of the advent of the European on the American continent took a long time to reach its ghastly conclusion—has yet, in fact, to do so. In truth, as a historical phenomenon, the Indian disintegrated; as an Indian he was not annihilated but he faded culturally into another entity. The crime, if there was one, was the inexorable breakdown of the native's cultural integrity, in part the result of conscious policy and in part the inevitable consequence of competition between two disparate ways of life. Rather than the singular clarity of one despicable act, the American aborigine was the victim of a process. Perhaps process can be criminal but its natural complexity diffuses the locus of guilt. Criminality tends to be individual and guilt is much more easily imputed when the criminal and his victim can be seen apart from circumstance or the slow, dissolving force of cultural breakdown. The moralistic impact falls more exactingly when the demarcation between the opposing forces is set off clearly. When Indian and white meet on equal terms and the white man brazenly violates most of the rules, or when the Indian, helpless before the overpowering force of civilization, is portrayed as the pitiable victim of aggression, the simplistic duality makes the assignment of guilt an easy task; but when the conflict is submerged in the process of cultural intermingling, the moralistic dichotomy dissolves. If only because it is virtually impossible to declare a whole society guilty, the moralistic approach requires an implicit denial of the integrity of culture, in effect, a shattering of the wholeness of that complex of experience and rational judgment from which men inevitably construct a style of life peculiar to themselves.

As a formalizing conception, the notion of integral culture[7] is freighted with the dangers of moral relativism. Anthropologists, ethnologists, and sociologists have long argued the matter to no great satisfaction. Historians seem even more open to the apparent dilemma of scholarly detachment and moral involvement. Certainly the conflict between Indian and white, deeply associated with civilized man's misgivings in the face of his primitive antithesis, has always conjured in the historical mind oppression and hypocrisy and has demanded a moral accounting. Robert Berkhofer, in his recent study of missionary activities among the Indians, carries the relativist perspective beyond the subject perceived into the very eye of the perceiver. "Current indictments of past American conduct," he writes, "are on the same plane as earlier American condemnations of savage society. The Americans of the past were victims of

---

[6] Foreman, *Indian Removal*, 386.

[7] My own understanding of the concept is taken in part from: A. L. Kroeber and Clyde Kluckhohn, *Culture: A Critical Review of Concepts and Definitions*, Vintage ed. (New York, 1963); Robert K. Merton, *Social Theory and Social Structure*, 3d ed., (New York, 1968), Chap. III; A. R. Radcliffe-Brown, *Structure and Function in Primitive Society: Essays and Addresses* (New York, 1952), Introduction, Chap. IX; T. S. Eliot, *Notes towards the Definition of Culture* (New York, 1949); Robert A. Nisbet, *The Sociological Tradition* (New York, 1966).

their cultural values just as their latter-
day judges are victims of today's beliefs."[8]
We are all, one supposes, witting or not,
in one degree or another, victims of our
nurture, but at least we recognize it, thus
saving the historian's capacity for judgment from the epistemological dead end
of consistent relativism. The concept of
integral culture should not reduce the
historian to a mere recorder; it should
only insure that judgments be qualified
by the peculiar circumstances of a distinct cultural definition. Ethics, the im-
puting of guilt or innocence, must not
be excluded from the process of historical
judgment but it must become much less
obtrusive. The issue of right or wrong
must give way to an understanding of the
process of cultural conflict that characterized the meeting of European and Indian in the New World. Cultural analysis
should be relativist only in the sense that
it is an inclusive conception, in the sense
that it allows the historian to see all the
intricate permeations of the intermeshing
of disparate cultures rather than the one-
to-one moral dichotomy of oppressor and
oppressed.

Practically, it should be enough to re-
furbish William N. Fenton's plea in 1953
that Indian-white relations be treated as
a common ground of history and ethnology . Little had been done when he wrote
to combine the two sources of knowledge,
that is, to examine Indian-white conflict
as a clash of culture, and little has been
done since. According to one historian of
the frontier, recent work in anthropology
and ethnology "has brought us much
closer to a satisfactory understanding"
of the character of native reaction to white

intrusion. Another makes the determined
pledge "to understand the life, the societies, the cultures, the thinking and feeling of the Indians."[9] The intentions are
the best and even the performance is
solid and enlightening. But it cannot be
said in any broad sense that Fenton's hope
has been fulfilled. We still await an account of Indian-white relations in the
early period that will bring to bear the
full weight of the knowledge of human
culture.

The best of the recent literature does
indeed make use of cultural analysis
though not usually to the extent of excluding the moralistic disjunction. A
notable exception is Wilbur R. Jacobs's
examination of frontier diplomacy in the
light of the native tradition of gift giving.
By centering upon the major form of
official contact between white and Indian
and pointing out its ceremonial significance for the native society, Jacobs adds
the sinews of culture to the bland confrontation between native and civilized
negotiators. Though perhaps the broad
subject of cultural conflict cannot be interpreted on the basis of so limited a
theme, the volume remains one of the
few recent efforts to lay out some of the
intricacies of Indian-white relations while
taking seriously the character of the native way of life. Surely, however, the
most successful attempt in the past generation, describing the consequences of
the infiltration of civilized manners into
primitive America, is Anthony F. C.
Wallace's biographical study of the Dela-
ware leader Teedyuscung. Through a

---

[8] Robert Berkhofer, Jr., *Salvation and the Savage:
An Analysis of Protestant Missions and American
Indian Response, 1787–1862* (Lexington, Ky., 1965),
ix.

[9] William N. Fenton, *American Indian and White
Relations to 1830: Needs & Opportunities for Study*
(Chapel Hill, 1957), 17; Douglas Edward Leach, *The
Northern Colonial Frontier, 1607–1763* (New York,
1966), 7; Louis De Vorsey, Jr., *The Indian Boundary
in the Southern Colonies, 1763–1775* (Chapel Hill,
1966), 43.

personality fatally undermined but rich in historical implications, Wallace examines the effect of civilization on the delicate structure of Indian culture.[10]

Of course there is much evidence in the recent literature that historians do take the integrity of the Indian's culture seriously. Reginald Horsman notes in more than one place the Indian's conscious determination to defend his own way of doing things against the inexorable push of advancing America. Louis De Vorsey, while conceding the rudimentary character of tribal political organization, maintains that "the Indians evinced a passionate desire to retain their territorial bases which they identified as vital to their continued existence as a people." In his account of the New England frontier, Alden Vaughan refers to the barriers of custom and language over which the Puritan missionaries could not prevail. But it is perhaps Berkhofer who sees most distinctly the Indian as a cultural entity. In perceiving that the cultural clash between missionary and native was total, that the missionary demanded nothing less from the Indian than a complete ethnic capitulation ("To become truly Christian was to become anti-Indian."), he broaches the question of the dynamics of cultural interplay. Though the white man's way of life operates, in this case as a culture-dissolving ideology, the Indian's manners and mores, in their gradual dissolution, are conceded a unique definition. The Indian and the white man are different because their experience

and historical adjustment to the surrounding world have been different. They come together in the inevitable clash and denouement and just as certain decline of the weaker, less resilient party. The totality of the conflict sharpens the conception of cultural differentiation.[11]

Paradoxically, the successes illustrate the failures. Though virtually every historian of Indian-white relations would agree to the need for a recognition of cultural distinctness as an essential part of his conceptual apparatus, few have been able to bring the idea into the actual complexities of cultural competition. It is virtually de rigueur for an author to make some formal pronouncement on the subject, but there seems to be no requirement that the ideas reach fruition. What one comes to expect still is a history of Indian-white contact told from the white man's side, the Indian playing the role of anonymous opponent or victim. Disintegration or acculturation is often noted, and approved or regretted but there is seldom any deep analysis of the processes. Civilization simply sweeps across the pages in triumph or ignominy and the Indian fights or dies with no more identity than any other expendable resource. If the conceptualization need not produce an extensive ethnological examination, it should at least qualify the tendency for moralistic division and manifest some sense of the consequences of cultural conflict.

Berkhofer, having laid down the most solid base for cultural relativism, suffers

---

[10] Wilbur R. Jacobs, *Wilderness Politics and Indian Gifts: The Northern Colonial Frontier, 1748–1763* (Lincoln, Neb., 1966); originally published as *Diplomacy and Indian Gifts: Anglo-French Rivalry along the Ohio and Northwest Frontiers, 1748–1763* (Stanford, 1950); Anthony F. C. Wallace, *King of the Delawares: Teedyuscung, 1700–1763* (Philadelphia, 1949).

[11] Reginald Horsman, *Expansion and American Indian Policy, 1783–1812* (East Lansing, Mich., 1967), 38, 60; Reginald Horsman, *Matthew Elliot, British Indian Agent* (Detroit, 1964), 39; De Vorsey, *The Indian Boundary*, 44; Alden T. Vaughan, *New England Frontier: Puritans and Indians, 1620–1675* (Boston, 1965), 298, 304; Berkhofer, *Salvation and the Savage*, 69, 107, 122.

most patently from the failure. As he writes, "psychologically speaking, there seemed to be no halfway point" for the Indians in their confrontation with civilization. The missionaries' ideology paid little heed to the complications of cultural transformation. They "did not know . . . that basic values change very slowly."[12] In taking his cue from the white man's mental disposition, Berkhofer never enters the arena in which the two societies meet. The missionaries try to supplant the native social order and fail because, as he aptly points out, their ideology takes no cognizance of the relative imperviousness of culture to change. Just so the historian, even though he is aware of the importance of cultural analysis, is unable to move beyond the sterile detachment of the white man's anti-cultural ideology. Cultural relativism, unless it leads to an analysis of the processes of societal transformation, will do no more than trace the outlines of a historiographical problem. It will not fill the empty space.

The older approach to Indian-white relations, which on principle paid little attention to cultural interplay, and portrayed the Indian as unwitting victim and the white man as conscienceless aggressor, apparently still has some steam left in it.

It is well enough that Leach should maintain that "we are now less interested in pointing the finger of guilt at one race or the other" or that Jacobs should caution us that in its own time the confrontation was not viewed "as the black-and-white moral issue which it often seems to us today." Wilcomb E. Washburn, however, will have none of such pussyfooting. In a vigorous and knowledgeable defense, he proclaims his strong sympathy for the American Indian and insists that historians must judge from the sources the relative weight of guilt or innocence in the story of Indian-white conflict. One cannot, as he says, "split the difference."[13]

The historian as distributor of censure has a far easier task if he may be permitted to abstract his subject from history and therefore from cultural analysis. And such has been the most frequently used method in assigning the burden of guilt to the white man. The Indian is enhanced in prestige by the simple expedient of being plucked from the cultural maelstrom. From the beginning of Indian-white contact the convention of the noble savage has acted primarily as a criterion of moral rectitude against which the transgressions of civilization might be judged. And it has always been an explicitly ahistorical concept, posited on a pre-Adamic definition of man. Washburn reveals a sympathy for just such an understanding of the Indian. He contends particularly that the natives manifested a natural hospitality toward the Europeans on first encounter and that violence was the fault of the whites. The Indian can be blamed only for retaliating against an original aggression. Indeed the noble savage convention

---

[12] *Ibid.*, 57, 111. Similarly, Roy Harvey Pearce, *The Savages of America: A Study of the Indian and the Idea of Civilization,* rev. ed. (Baltimore, 1965), in an often brilliant exposition of the content of the white man's mind on the subject of the Indian, is not able to stretch his account to cover the interplay of the two societies. Since his thesis is that the native was perceived mainly with reference to the white man's conception of himself, he does not step over and treat the Indian on his own ground. The validity of the thesis is not in question but the assumption that ideology can be so pristine and self-contained is another problem. The direct effect of the white man's conception, as Pearce admits, is the manipulation of the Indian and, therefore, even civilization's intellectual inversions concerning native society may be seen as part of the interplay of culture.

[13] Leach, *The Northern Colonial Frontier,* 7; Wilbur R. Jacobs, ed., *The Paxton Riots and the Frontier Theory* (Chicago, 1967), 1; Wilcomb E. Washburn, ed., *The Indian and the White Man* (Garden City, N.Y., 1964), xi.

itself stems from the first reports of this aboriginal good will.[14] In fact noble savagism had long been a part of the paradisaic strain in Western thought and did not grow out of the observations of early explorers and settlers. They brought the idea with them but were undoubtedly pleased for a new field in which to apply it.[15] At the same time it is entirely possible that European society had a higher violence quotient than the Indian's way of life; the white man was, after all, more adept. Of far more importance is the prognosis for historical understanding on the basis of a blatantly non-historical original assumption. A history of Indian-white relations must take its beginning in the admission of the Indian's peculiar cultural composition, itself the product of history. It can gain nothing, and it might well lose everything, by proposing a mythic natural innocence and proceeding to direct thunderbolts at those who supposedly despoiled it.

Despite his predilection for moral history, however, Washburn does not propose a consistent utilization of the noble savage theme in interpreting Indian-white relations. He defines noble savagery with a list of primitive attributes, "generosity, stoic bearing of pain, dignity, loftiness of speech in council," all of which are common properties of Edenic man. But for him they are merely the norms of a noble Indian society.[16] He comes back finally to a cultural conception but his determination to assign moral blame leads him to impose on it the ends usually expected from the noble savage convention. The methodological ambiguity of such an approach can only cast doubt on the ultimate conclusions.

Though less abstracted than the primitivism of the noble savage concept, there has long been a tendency in Western thought to see human nature as a static, universal quality. Only the accidents of existence change; at the core of the human organism there remains a stable, predictable essence. Thus arguments for equality and human dignity usually have their basis in a timeless realm of moral value. In a practical sense, it is frequently difficult for the historian to see the complex of motive and action in a peculiar culture as in its root different from that of another style of existence. Besides the inhibitions of the historian's own ethnocentrism, he is usually forced to come to terms with a universalist ideology that constantly nudges him toward a static explanation of behavior.

In attempting to unravel the intricacies of the Indian-white relationship, therefore, the historian is tempted frequently to judge both sides against the same set of expectations. The Indian behaves as the white man does and for the same reasons. Of course there is some merit in the procedure. The Indian was far more affected

---

[14] Wilcomb E. Washburn, "The Moral and Legal Justifications for Dispossessing the Indians," in James Morton Smith, ed., *Seventeenth Century America: Essays in Colonial History* (Chapel Hill, 1959), 22; Washburn, ed., *The Indian and the White Man*, xii, 415. Nancy Oestreich Lurie, "Indian Cultural Adjustment to European Civilization," in Smith, ed., *Seventeenth Century America*, 36–38, offers an explanation of the Indians' hospitable greeting of the Virginia settlers without recourse to any version of the noble savage theme.

[15] Henri Baudet, *Paradise on Earth: Some Thoughts on European Images of Non-European Man*, Elizabeth Wentholt, transl. (New Haven, 1965).

[16] Wilcomb E. Washburn, "A Moral History of Indian-White Relations: Needs and Opportunities for Study," *Ethnohistory*, IV (1957), 55. An admirably perceptive treatment of relations between the Indian and one particular group of whites is in Lewis O. Saum, *The Fur Trader and the Indian* (Seattle, 1965). He contends that fur traders, frequently skirting the formulations of noble savagism (p. 80), managed to come up with a generally realistic conception of the native. "The more the trader saw of the Indian the greater were his misgivings." (p. 134)

by the white than the white by the Indian. He began absorbing the ways of civilization at first contact, sometimes even before a face-to-face meeting. But the Indian was not a blank tablet; even in the process of acculturation there remained a substratum of Indian character. He was always an Indian and the whites were frequently reminded of it. The truth of the matter will be out when the historian can tell at any given moment the level of Indianness in his subject—when, in effect, he can judge the extent of acculturation.

Doubtless such a demand is beyond the capacity of the historical science. Yet it is also questionable that analysis should be stopped at a mere recitation of the particular changes instituted in Indian society under the influence of civilization. If Berkhofer explained little about the processes of historical change in defining the totalism of the missionary ideology, Mary Young does not reveal more in listing the positive changes begun under missionary auspices. The introduction of civilized medicine, the discouragement of dancing and ball play, the elimination of elaborate and prolonged mourning, and the attack on polygamy, infanticide, whiskey drinking, and obscene conversation, all bore heavily on the alteration of native society, but, surely, not all to the same degree, and the cancellation of one white-induced habit, whiskey drinking, might well have meant a return to the old ways.[17] Breaking into a dynamic situation at a given point, without considering the subtle process of change, as in any still life, risks distortion. One is inclined, as a consequence, to weigh the quantity of change without detecting its vital quality.

Still more serious is the practice of im-puting characteristics of the white man's culture to the Indians, as, for example, Francis Paul Prucha's contention that the "elemental question" between the two societies was "who was to own and control the land."[18] To be sure, the white man wanted the land and the Indian opposed him sometimes, but little has really been said about the nature of the conflict unless the position of land (even the concept takes its meaning from civilization) is laid out in the differing value systems of the two societies. The land can be accounted the basic point of conflict only if it can be shown that the Indian had a sense of spatial identity similar to the white man's. He did not, or at least there is no reason to think that he did. He did not do the same things to land that the white man did. If he sometimes manifested the jealous attachment to it that the whites were wont to expect, he certainly gave much of it up without more than a perfunctory struggle—assuming that he even understood what was meant by giving it up. Also, as the Indian came to see the white man's intense desire for the land and as he felt the effects of the civilized invasion of his own cultural sphere—which was, in effect, the white man taking the land—he came also to see that he had to preserve his territorial integrity. This, however, was more likely the consequence of acculturation than a primitive allegiance to a plot of soil. The issue was not so much the land as the disintegration of the native's culture which led finally to his sturdy defense of his territorial possessions. Whatever the explanation, it must avoid a formulation of values based

[17] Mary Elizabeth Young, *Redskins, Ruffleshirts, and Rednecks: Indian Land Allotments in Alabama and Mississippi, 1830–1860* (Norman, 1961), 24-25.

[18] Francis Paul Prucha, *American Indian Policy in the Formative Years: The Indian Trade and Intercourse Acts, 1790–1834* (Cambridge, Mass., 1962), 139; Horsman, *Expansion and American Indian Policy,* Introduction, makes the same point on the relation of land to Indian-white conflict.

on one culture without considering the interplay of different value systems.

Similarly Jacobs speaks of an Indian "war for independence" and of an essentially democratic government and individualist spirit. Allen Trelease uses such terms with reference to Indian society as "public opinion," "anarchy," and an "oligarchic body of sachems." Fenton seems to think it possible that the Iroquois federation served as archetype for the federal constitution. And Alvin M. Josephy, Jr., using Franklin's exasperated but quite conventional comparison of the supposed political accomplishments of the Indians and the ingrained divisiveness of the colonies, maintains that the Iroquois league had an "indirect" influence on the establishment of the union and the structure of the new government in 1789. Furthermore, he contends, these politically astute aborigines can be described with at least partial accuracy in the conventional wisdom of noble savagery. They believed in the "freedom and dignity of the individual" and relied on unanimous vote in their councils to preserve the "equality of individuals and respect for their rights." Such transference of the clichés of the white man's political rhetoric cannot but do violence to the Indian's cultural integrity. There is no dignity in the Indian impersonating the white man.[19]

More pertinent is the treatment of the Indian as warrior and diplomatist. Since a fair portion of the story of Indian-white relations is taken up with the proceedings of war and the making of peace, most authors are forced to commit themselves, at least implicitly, to a rationale for dealing with the subject. Indeed no problems are more difficult of explanation than the motives which impelled the savages to violence and determined their objects in ending it. The great danger to the historian is in attributing to the Indian the rational detachment in external politics that would be expected from a civilized statesman. Perhaps the two best examples are Parkman's account of Pontiac as a potential builder of a forest empire and George T. Hunt's economic explanation of Iroquois belligerence.[20]

Trelease deals with the question of Iroquois motivation in his book on seventeenth-century Indian affairs in New York. A cautious historian, he approaches the matter with some trepidation. Though the Indians, he thinks, did not necessarily have the same motives as the whites, there is as much reason to attribute economic incentive to them as there is to civilized man. Before the arrival of the European, the Indians fought for various reasons, but with the beginning of the fur trade economics became paramount.[21] Without question, then, the European demand for furs and the Indian's willingness to supply them created a convenient barter nexus between the two societies—a decidedly economic relationship. But outside of Manchester there is no purely economic condition. The key is in the

---

[19] Jacobs, *Wilderness Politics and Indian Gifts,* 13-14, 185, n. 143; Allen W. Trelease, *Indian Affairs in Colonial New York: The Seventeenth Century* (Ithaca, 1960), 22; Fenton, *American Indian and White Relations to 1830,* 18, 27; Alvin M. Josephy, Jr., *The Indian Heritage of America* (New York, 1968), 34-35; see also Alvin M. Josephy, Jr., *The Patriot Chiefs: A Chronicle of American Indian Leadership* (New York, 1961), 28-29.

[20] Francis Parkman, *The Conspiracy of Pontiac . . .* (Boston [orig. pub., Boston, 1851], 1898), I, 190–198; for an alternate explanation, see Howard H. Peckham, *Pontiac and the Indian Uprising* (Chicago, 1961), 107–108, n. 12; George T. Hunt, *The Wars of the Iroquois: A Study of Intertribal Trade Relations* (Madison [orig. pub. Madison, 1940], 1960), 32–37; see the review by Fenton in *American Anthropologist,* New Ser., XLII (1940), 662–664.

[21] Trelease, *Indian Affairs in Colonial New York,* 53.

cultural context, the effect of the white man's artifacts on Indian society. The Indian's dependence was not economic, it was cultural. Any explanation must deal with the peculiar ecological and cultural changes induced by the spreading of the white man's wares through the forest.

The Iroquois portrayed by Trelease are far more self-contained than might be expected, though it is difficult to deny them their continued talent in wilderness politics even after their life had been seriously affected by the inroads of a foreign culture. The Five Nations prove their independence, writes Trelease, in choosing to move into the west for their own purposes; their attack on the Huron is a conscious tribal policy. (A similar calculation can be seen in the activities of the Algonquin Indians in the Peach War of 1655.) The Iroquois' prudence is illustrated in their determination not to expand the conflict to the Abenaki when they were already at war with the French; and their diplomatic nimbleness when, at least on one occasion, they were able to outmaneuver both the French and the British.[22] Now in any of its parts it is not really an unlikely story; Trelease tells a sensible tale and he writes from the sources. However, it is the accumulation, the piling up of evidence of native ability that tends finally to draw the two societies apart. The situation changes from the subtle intermingling of disparate cultures to the confrontation of two sovereign powers, both jealous of their independence, and both fully equipped to maintain it. The treatment of Indian-white relations through the medium of foreign policy leads invariably to the neglect of the cultural process.

But, even aside from the relative emphasis on the cultural approach, it seems

that the white man's policy toward the Indian is in the throes of reinterpretation. There appear still such treatments as William T. Hagan's overview of the Indian in American history, more concerned with gratuitous slurs against the white than the thoughtful understanding of the meeting of the two societies, or R. S. Cotterill's essay in sarcasm on the five southern tribes.[23] In two recent volumes, however, the history of American Indian-white relations has taken an important step beyond the guilt-ridden accounts of the past. At one end of the period, Alden T. Vaughan on Puritan-Indian relations in the seventeenth century and, at the other end, Francis Paul Prucha on government Indian policy in the early national period, have provided the basis for a different perspective on the subject.

Vaughan's effort is a disarming defense of the Puritan treatment of the New England natives. On the whole the Puritans were "humane, considerate, and just," and "had a surprisingly high regard for the interests of a people who were less

---

[22] *Ibid.*, 118–120, 141–142, 260, 266–267, 299.

[23] William T. Hagan, *American Indians* (Chicago, 1961), takes every opportunity to see the worst in the white man's action. "Traders employed any tactics to make an immediate profit" (p. 16); intermarriage was intended merely to further the economic and political objectives of the whites (p. 12); a "double standard of morality" was used by whites in dealing with Indians (p. 20); Indian students at William and Mary were "supported by charity and instructed in segregated classes." (pp. 10–11) Worse yet, during the Revolution "two Indians killed were partially flayed to provide boot tops for the troops as addicted to souvenir-hunting as their twentieth century counterparts." (p. 38) And Tecumseh, so the report goes, "was flayed and his skin made into souvenir razor strops by the representatives of the higher way of life." (p. 63) The Indian is merely victim and the white man only oppressor. R. S. Cotterill, *The Southern Indians: The Story of the Civilized Tribes before Removal* (Norman, 1954), 124, 139–140, 153, 174, 224; a particularly cavalier and simplistic description of Jeffersonian policy may be found in Marshall Smelser, *The Democratic Republic, 1801–1815* (New York, 1968), 132–134.

powerful, less civilized, less sophisticated, and—in the eyes of the New England colonists—less godly." Though doubtless their kind of violence was more intense, they employed it less frequently than the Indians. Rather than bringing chaos to New England, the Puritans were the only power capable of keeping the peace among the volatile tribes. In the two major Indian-white conflicts, with the Pequots and later against King Philip, the Puritans dealt devastating blows to Indian power but they did not cause the fighting. In the first, the Pequots, themselves intruders, must take the blame and in the second the impetus for war came not from the Puritans but from Philip in his fear for the loss of his prestige and power.[24]

Vaughan is not unsympathetic to the Indian. He simply believes that the Puritan attitude toward them was worthy of praise. The two societies did not really clash; it was merely that the one was "unified, visionary, disciplined, and dynamic" while the other was "self-satisfied, undisciplined, and static."[25] One knows, however, whose side he has chosen. The Puritans expanded, as was the European habit, into the sphere of the Indians. Since what the Indians did in a certain location cannot really be called occupying the land, at least not in the sense that the whites did, Puritan society gradually moved in and took over. It is not just a question of physical displacement though there was much of that; the Puritans did purchase land from the Indians. Rather the process was more an imperceptible cultural advance by the Puritans and recession by the Indians.

Thus in his conclusions Vaughan communicates a sense of the process of the Indian's cultural decline. But the bulk of his book contains no such impression. In overturning the critical view of the white man and in raising the estimation of the Puritan's intentions, he dwells on the theme of positive policy. The Indian and Puritan, finally, are treated as equals, dealing with one another over the vital issues of war, peace, trade, religion, and social conviviality. The Indian, having a sound notion of the meaning of land possession, sells it, most often willingly, to the Puritan. The law of civilization is accepted by the native people as an equitable means of arranging for a mutually satisfactory juridical condition. The Puritans introduce themselves into a complex extra-tribal political situation as one more power among equals.[26] In his recounting of the story, Vaughan does not really break into the cultural interplay of Indian-white relations. It is not merely because he willingly uses only Puritan sources (all the historical sources, after all, are the white man's) but that he fails to take the Indian on his own terms. Indian society, as he notes, is "divided, self-satisfied, undisciplined, and static": all antivirtues in Protestant civilization's hierarchy of value. The great defect of the Puritan in dealing with the Indian (with any other people, for that matter) was his inability to see the external world through any other glass but his own, and that darkly. If on the whole the Puritan did his best for the Indian, as a good Christian it was only expected of him, but he did not concede the Indian a cultural separateness and integrity. Vaughan has disposed of the guilty white man scheme,

---

[24] Vaughan, *New England Frontier,* vii–viii, 78, 136–137, 183–184, 312–313. Douglas Edward Leach, *Flintlock and Tomahawk: New England in King Philip's War* (New York [orig. pub., New York, 1958], 1966), 14–22, blames the conflict on the Puritan pressure for land.

[25] Vaughan, *New England Frontier,* 323.

[26] *Ibid.,* 104–109, 155, 183, 210.

but just as the Puritans had, he does not act on the recognition that the two societies really were different.

Culminating with the removal policy and the revision of the trade and intercourse acts of 1834, Prucha presents a compelling account of the policy of the young nation toward the natives. His sympathy for the Indian is manifest, but he offers a rounded and perceptive portrayal of the white man's struggle to deal with the confrontation of the two societies. Though his perspective is dictated by his emphasis on policy, he is sensibly aware of the clash of culture, especially of the decline of the Indian under the influence of civilization, and he is chary of distributing blame. Perhaps the major revision in the volume is contained in chapter nine: "Civilization and Removal." The very title hurls defiance at an interpretation long accepted by historians. Removal, after all, has been considered the *locus classicus* of Indian-white relations as a "suffering situation." It was the last outrage heaped by the merciless white man on the heads of the much abused eastern Indians. Prucha's motive in coupling removal with the effort to civilize the Indian is clearly to metamorphose the argument from the one-level "trail of tears" to the complicated interplay of the white man's interest and conscience on the one side and the painful acculturation of a primitive society on the other. He admits, of course, that there was a sufficiency of nefarious motives behind the decision to drive the Indians west of the Mississippi but maintains that not enough attention has been paid to the good motives of those who made government policy in the second and third decades of the nineteenth century. The crucial point is the decision of such men as Thomas L. McKenney, Lewis Cass, and William Clark that the civilizing program had failed, that the major effect of the white man on the Indian was deleterious rather than improving, and that the native could be saved only by removing him from harm's way. Beyond the Mississippi, out of reach of the corrosive elements in the white man's way of life, he could be preserved and possibly civilized before the next advance of American society rolled over him. Removal for many who approached the Indian from the highest philanthropy was "another program for the 'preservation and civilization' of the aborigines."[27]

Prucha's case is well taken; the oppressor-victim interpretation, after all, will not explain why men of generally laudable character favored removal. Placing it in the context of civilized philanthropy and Indian disintegration tells something of the way two disparate societies meet and come finally to terms with each other. But Prucha's intentions are limited. He is dealing with policy and the immediate motives leading to its formulation. Except for noting the dawning perception of the consequences of civilization on the Indian, he is not really concerned with the question of cultural interplay. And, indeed, a definition of policy without digging into the substratum of culture that

---

[27] Prucha, *American Indian Policy*, 224–227. But aside from Prucha, it is virtually impossible to find a treatment of removal that sees it as an extension of the civilizing effort. Most historians conceive of the two policies as contradictory and evidence of the hypocrisy or stupidity of the whites. See Horsman, *Expansion and American Indian Policy*, 109–111, 116–117, 140; Hagan, *American Indians*, 44, 54; Young, *Redskins, Ruffleshirts, and Rednecks*, 5–6, 9; R. Pierce Beaver, *Church, State, and the American Indians: Two and a Half Centuries of Partnership in Missions between Churches and Government* (St. Louis, 1966), 90, 99–100, 117; Cotterill, *The Southern Indians*, 225–226. A recent Book-of-the-Month-Club Selection, Peter Farb, *Man's Rise to Civilization as Shown by the Indians of North America from Primeval Times to the Coming of the Industrial State* (New York, 1968), 250, calls the removal policy "genocide" and compares it to the Nuremburg Laws.

rests beneath it will not yield an interpretation of Indian-white relations that brings together all the elements of cultural differentiation. Yet in showing that there was more to the white man's actions than viciousness, greed, and hypocrisy, he has opened a broad vista for historical imagination.

Horsman supplies the theme of American expansion as an introduction to his account of Indian-white relations in the early years of the nation. The Indian was overwhelmed by a new thriving people but not without a lingering sense of the wickedness of the proceeding. Americans were caught by the incompatibility of their interests (a growing population, the attraction of the fertile west, national feeling, and the need for strategic protection), and their conscience (the righteousness of the Revolution and the uniqueness of the American experiment) which in the face of Indian opposition could not produce a realistic policy.[28] The good will of the white man, then, as manifested in the civilizing program, appears as an inconsequential quirk, an aberration when the reality was removal. The pieces are all there but Horsman's division seems arbitrary. The thrust of the white man's culture, more likely, had an essential unity. The philanthropic determination to civilize the Indian was as much a part of an expanding America as greed for land and removal. The danger in assuming a contradiction between civilization and removal is that the first inevitably becomes a sham and the second merely positive evidence of the white man's callousness. Similarly, it tends to transpose the question out of the realm of cultural conflict. If the Indian was destroyed by the onrush of European culture then philanthropy must be seen as one instrument in the Indian's gradual demise. As Prucha so aptly puts it: "It was a question of civilization versus the savage state, and no one was ready to preach that savagism should be perpetuated."[29] Horsman's extension of the interpretation into an examination of the forces of American expansion together with Prucha's association of removal with the civilizing program constitute a significant move towards the understanding of Indian-white relations as a problem in cultural conflict. Both the source of the white man's overpowering influence on the fragile structure of native society and the subtle operations of civilization's best intentioned philanthropy are thrown open to scrutiny.

Implicit in the suffering-Indian, wicked white-man interpretation is the proposition that the American aborigine could have survived. The vague assumption is that things might have been different, that the white man should have been less pushy, that the Indian might have been better protected, that the treaties should

---

[28] Horsman, *Expansion and American Indian Policy,* Introduction, 172–173.

[29] Prucha, *American Indian Policy,* 239; Pearce, *Savages of America,* ix, 3–4, 41–42, 73–74, also emphasizes the division between savagism and civilization. He contends that after the middle of the eighteenth century the native was looked on mainly as an obstacle to civilization's advance. And hence civilizing the Indian was one way of mastering him, of overcoming an obstacle to progress. Leslie A. Fiedler, *The Return of the Vanishing American* (New York, 1968), 76, offers a typically racy but apt version of the essential unity of the white man's treatment of the Indian: "Not quite destroying, really, for the act of genocide with which our nation began was inconclusive, imperfect, inhibited by a bad conscience, undercut by uncertainty of purpose. 'There's no good injun but a dead injun,' the really principled killers, which is to say, the soldiers, cried; but, 'The next best thing is a Christian Indian,' the softhearted castrators, which is to say, the Priests, reminded them; and, 'We can get along with *any* Indian, so long as he's on the Reservation,' the practical-minded ghettoizers, which is to say, the bureaucrats and social workers, advised them both—having final say."

have been kept, that, finally, the Indian could have endured as an Indian. As a moral injunction the idea takes on certain pristine clarity but it says little about the interplay of culture. Without drifting into the bog of historical inevitability, it must be said that any rearrangement of the forces of Indian-white relations in the early period does little to improve the native's chances. Perhaps a slowing of the white man's advance, some accommodation on median issues, even palliation of the native's suffering, a gentler demise, but whether the Indian was annihilated or transformed, he would no longer be an Indian. Short of abandoning the Mississippi Valley, says Horsman, there seems no reason to think that the problem could have been solved. The "stark realities," writes Leach, dictated that the native society had to submit. Even Hagan, speaking of the Cherokees, believes their case was hopeless.[30]

The consequences of Indian-white confrontation, the passing of a culture, are, however, too cosmic to be without a villain. The unruly frontiersman, fresh from years of Turnerian adulation, must now bear a major portion of the guilt for the Indian's destruction. As agent of American expansion, the wily and undisciplined pioneer, year after year, despite repeated governmental efforts to curb him, pushed the line of white settlement farther into the Indian country.[31] He was the practical surrogate of the white man's brash and aggressive society as it met and proceeded to accomplish the demolition of the native culture. The frontiersman could have been curbed only if the very nature of America could have been

qualified; to stem the advance would have meant, conversely, to impair the very vitality of the white man's society. Besides attributing to the societal phenomenon an unrealistic level of rational discipline, the contention that order could have been imposed on the frontier assumes the existence of a bureaucratic and military establishment of far greater size and proficiency than circumstances would permit. The government could not have built a Chinese Wall, as Washington put it, to keep the whites and Indians apart.[32] Even the supposed guilt of the frontiersman will not assuage the historiographical decisiveness of the situation; within the terms available for explanation, the Indian's transformation was inevitable.

As mere sentiment the hope for the Indian's survival removes the encounter between white and native from the dynamics of historical process, but it reveals also an unspoken rationalism which, when applied to history, supposes that society is capable of a self-articulation far beyond realistic expectation. A society manifesting such detachment, revealing fully its own inner workings, and thereby judging the effect it might have on another culture, would be a rare phenomenon. Doubtless, in every age there are some who are able to see a fair portion of the intricate patterns of their society and they are sometimes successful in convincing a fraction of their fellows of the accuracy of the vision. But the limitations of rational articulation and control are compounded when the society is as lacking in coherence as colonial and early national America. It was not merely a question of a shortage of governmental or philanthropic goodwill but of a boom-

[30] Horsman, *Expansion and American Indian Policy*, 173; Leach, *The Northern Colonial Frontier*, 190; Hagan, *American Indians*, 76.

[31] Prucha, *American Indian Policy*, 3, 143–144, 147, 162.

[32] George Washington to Timothy Pickering, July 1, 1796, John C. Fitzpatrick, ed., *The Writings of George Washington ...* (Washington, 1931–1944), XXXV, 112.

ing white America bursting out of the constrictions of its social bounds, causing the decline of a native society virtually devoid of the resources for serious competition. The white man is guilty only if one supposes his society capable of a total transmogrification into an entity of mature social discipline, able to establish settled and well-defined relations with its fragile neighbor. There was as much possibility for such a cosmic alteration as there was that the Indian would suddenly develop the cultural muscle to withstand the effects of the white man's aggressiveness. Of course, neither the one nor the other was conceivable. The pattern of interrelation between white and Indian, at least in its limits, was set by the integral nature of the two cultures and its history can be written only by accepting its tragic implications for the Indian and proceeding to the business of analyzing the cultural clash between the two societies. One need not sanction the self-righteousness of the white man's society or see any merit in the disheveled individualism that underlay its rush for conquest to understand the Indian's desperate situation. The process of his decline derives no meaning from the assertion of the white man's guilt; without the context of cultural disintegration the accusation is gratuitous. Within that context, however, it takes on a fitting pathos.

To be sure, the concept of integral culture is at base ethnological, but it is also historical. In the deepest sense there is no history that is not cultural history. Any other conception separates man from his existential dimension. Though a wide knowledge of ethnology would be of incalculable value in the study of Indian-white confrontation, what is more important is the sensitive perception that the human condition, civilized or savage, is always a pattern of intricately connected elements, that the pattern has its limits, and that the limits set off one society from another. For historical research the concept is self-validating. The investigation of governmental policy toward the Indian will develop against the content of American society and its political organization. An account of the native's adjustment to the influx of civilized artifacts will unfold according to the aborigine's ability to absorb or repel them, or conversely, it will describe the eroding effects of the importation of such foreign elements. In the interweaving of the two, in the meeting of the two disparate social orders, the concept of integral culture is of supreme importance. A model of what may be done is Eric R. Wolfe's *Sons of the Shaking Earth*,[33] an account of the clash of Indian and Spanish culture in middle America. Though based on wide ethnological study, the volume is a perceptive combination of cultural analysis and historical evolution. From the very origins of the land and humankind in the New World, he carries the story to the ascendant warrior kingdoms at the arrival of the Spaniards in the sixteenth century. The native culture, tense and precarious in its grip on life, proved no match for the Europeans who came fully prepared to impose their own ways on the Indian population. Paradoxically, the Spaniards also came in search of a paradise that would fill an elusive deficiency in their own psychic make-up. In bringing together all the strands of competitive interplay between native and European culture and superimposing the anti-culture of the Spaniards paradisaic ideology, Wolfe goes to the heart of the dynamics of human development.

Above all the Indian must be perceived as an Indian. Justice can be done him

---

[33] Eric R. Wolfe, *Sons of the Shaking Earth* (Chicago, 1959).

historically only if his special character is admitted. If he turns out to be only a vague reflection of the white man's wish for what he sees as best in himself—an idealized white man—or even if it is assumed that his behavior as a historical character can be judged by the objective definitions applied to civilized man, then the Indian will never be portrayed with the integrity he deserves. If his death is to be tragic, it must be the death of his real self, not of a white impostor.

Andrew Jackson has become the symbol of the Indian-hating American, and he has been severely condemned by historians for his removal of the Indians to the West. A new investigation of Jackson's Indian policy by FRANCIS PAUL PRUCHA (b. 1921) presents a different view. Expanding a position first set forth in his book, *American Indian Policy in the Formative Years* (1962), he argues that removal was a reasonable answer to the Indian problem facing Jackson and his contemporaries, not simply a ruthless dispossession of the Indians. Do his arguments overturn the conclusions of such critics as Van Every?*

Francis Paul Prucha

Andrew Jackson's Indian Policy

A great many persons—not excluding some notable historians—have adopted a "devil theory" of American Indian policy. And in their demonic hierarchy Andrew Jackson has first place. He is depicted primarily, if not exclusively, as a western frontiersman and famous Indian fighter, who was a zealous advocate of dispossessing the Indians and at heart an "Indian-hater." When he became President, the story goes, he made use of his new power, ruthlessly and at the point of a bayonet, to force the Indians from their ancestral homes in the East into desert lands west of the Mississippi, which were considered forever useless to the white man.

This simplistic view of Jackson's Indian policy is unacceptable. It was not Jackson's aim to crush the Indians because, as an old Indian fighter, he hated Indians. Although his years in the West had brought him into frequent contact with the Indians, he by no means developed a doctrinaire anti-Indian attitude. Rather, as a military man, his dominant goal in the decades before he became President was to preserve the security and well-being of the United States and its Indian and white inhabitants. His military experience, indeed, gave him an overriding concern for the safety of the nation from foreign rather than internal enemies, and to some extent the anti-Indian sentiment that has been charged against Jackson in his early career was instead basically anti-British. Jackson, as his first biographer pointed out, had "many private reasons for disliking" Great Britain. "In her, he could

* Francis Paul Prucha, "Andrew Jackson's Indian Policy: A Reassessment," *Journal of American History,* LVI (December, 1969), 527–539. Footnotes omitted.

trace the efficient cause, why, in early life, he had been left forlorn and wretched, without a single relation in the world." His frontier experience, too, had convinced him that foreign agents were behind the raised tomahawks of the red men. In 1808, after a group of settlers had been killed by the Creeks, Jackson told his militia troops: "[T]his brings to our recollection the horrid barbarity committed on our frontier in 1777 under the influence of and by the orders of Great Britain, and it is presumeable that the same influence has excited those barbarians to the late and recent acts of butchery and murder. . . ." From that date on there is hardly a statement by Jackson about Indian dangers that does not aim sharp barbs at England. His reaction to the Battle of Tippecanoe was that the Indians had been "excited to war by the secrete agents of Great Britain."

Jackson's war with the Creeks in 1813–1814, which brought him his first national military fame, and his subsequent demands for a large cession of Creek lands were part of his concern for security in the West. In 1815, when the Cherokees and Chickasaws gave up their overlapping claims to lands within the Creek cession, Jackson wrote with some exultation to Secretary of War James Monroe: "This Territory added to the creek cession, opens an avenue to the defence of the lower country, in a political point of view incalculable." A few months later he added: "The sooner these lands are brought into markett, [the sooner] a permanant security will be given to what, I deem, the most important, as well as the most vulnarable part of the union. This country once settled, our fortifications of defence in the lower country compleated, all [E]urope will cease to look at it with an eye to conquest. There is no other point of the union (america united) that com-bined [E]urope can expect to invade with success."

Jackson's plans with regard to the Indians in Florida were governed by similar principles of security. He wanted "to concentrate and locate the F[lorida] Indians at such a point as will promote their happiness and prosperity and at the same time, afford to that Territory a dense population between them and the ocean which will afford protection and peace to all." On later occasions the same views were evident. When negotiations were under way with the southern Indians for removal, Jackson wrote: "[T]he chickasaw and choctaw country are of great importance to us in the defence of the lower country [;] a white population instead of the Indian, would strengthen our own defence much." And again: "This section of country is of great importance to the prosperity and strength of the lower Mississippi[;] a dense white population would add much to its safety in a state of war, and it ought to be obtained, if it can, on anything like reasonable terms."

In his direct dealings with the Indians, Jackson insisted on justice toward both hostile and peaceful Indians. Those who committed outrages against the whites were to be summarily punished, but the rights of friendly Indians were to be protected. Too much of Jackson's reputation in Indian matters has been based on the first of these positions. Forthright and hard-hitting, he adopted a no-nonsense policy toward hostile Indians that endeared him to the frontiersmen. For example, when a white woman was taken captive by the Creeks, he declared: "With such arms and supplies as I can obtain I shall penetrate the creek Towns, until the Captive, with her Captors are delivered up, and think myself Justifiable, in laying waste their villiages, burning their houses, killing their warriors and leading into Captivity their wives and children, untill I do obtain a surrender of the Captive, and the Captors." In his general orders to the Tennessee militia after he received news of the Fort Mims massacre, he called for "retaliatory vengeance" against the "inhuman blood thirsty barbarians." He could speak of the "lex taliones," and his aggressive campaign against the Creeks and his escapade in Florida in the First Seminole War are further indications of his mood.

But he matched this attitude with one of justice and fairness, and he was firm in upholding the rights of the Indians who lived peaceably in friendship with the Americans. One of his first official acts as major general of the Tennessee militia was to insist on the punishment of a militia officer who instigated or at least permitted the murder of an Indian. On another occasion, when a group of Tennessee volunteers robbed a friendly Cherokee, Jackson's wrath burst forth: "that a sett of men should without any authority rob a man who is claimed as a member of the Cherokee nation, who is now friendly and engaged with us in a war against the hostile creeks, is such an outrage, to the rules of war, the laws of nations and of civil society, and well calculated to sower the minds of the whole nation against the united States, and is such as ought to meet with the frowns of every good citizen, and the agents be promptly prosecuted and punished as robers." It was, he said, as much theft as though the property had been stolen from a white citizen. He demanded an inquiry in order to determine whether any commissioned officers had been present or had had any knowledge of this "atrocious act," and he wanted the officers immediately arrested, tried by court-martial, and then turned over to the civil authority.

Again, during the Seminole War, when Georgia troops attacked a village of friendly Indians, Jackson excoriated the governor for "the base, cowardly and inhuman attack, on the old woman [women] and men of the chehaw village, whilst the Warriors of that *village* was with me, fighting the battles of our *country* against the common enemy." It was strange, he said, "that there could exist within the U. States, a cowardly monster in human shape, that could violate the sanctity of a flag, when borne by any person, but more particularly when in the hands of a superanuated Indian chief worn down with age. Such base cowardice and murderous conduct as this transaction affords, has not its paralel in history and should meet with its merited punishment." Jackson ordered the arrest of the officer who was responsible and declared: "This act will to the last ages fix a stain upon the character of Georgia."

Jackson's action as commander of the Division of the South in removing white squatters from Indian lands is another proof that he was not oblivious to Indian rights. When the Indian Agent Return J. Meigs in 1820 requested military assistance in removing intruders on Cherokee lands, Jackson ordered a detachment of twenty men under a lieutenant to aid in the removal. After learning that the officer detailed for the duty was "young and inexperienced," he sent his own aide-de-camp, Captain Richard K. Call, to assume command of the troops and execute the order of removal. "Captain Call informs me," he wrote in one report to Secretary of War John C. Calhoun, "that much noise of opposition was threatened, and men collected for the purpose who seperated on the approach of the regulars, but who threaten to destroy the cherokees in the Valley as soon as these Troops are gone. Capt. Call has addressed a letter to those infatuated people, with assurance of speedy and exemplary punishment if they should attempt to carry their threats into execution." Later he wrote that Call had performed his duties "with both judgement, and prudence and much to the interest of the Cherokee-Nation" and that the action would "have the effect in future of preventing the infraction of our Treaties with that Nation."

To call Jackson an Indian-hater or to declare that he believed that "the only good Indian is a dead Indian" is to speak in terms that had little meaning to Jackson. If is true, of course, that he did not consider the Indians to be noble savages. He had, for example, a generally uncomplimentary view of their motivation, and he argued that it was necessary to operate upon their fears, rather than on some higher motive. Thus, in 1812 he wrote: "I believe self interest and self preservation the most predominant passion. [F]ear is better than love with an indian." Twenty-five years later, just after he left the presidency, the same theme recurred; and he wrote: "long experience satisfies me that they are only to be well governed by their fears. If we feed their avarice we accelerate the causes of their destruction. By a prudent exertion of our military power we may yet do something to alleviate their condition at the same time that we certainly take from them the means of injury to our frontier."

Yet Jackson did not hold that Indians were inherently evil or inferior. He eagerly used Indian allies, personally liked and respected individual Indian chiefs, and, when (in the Creek campaign) an orphaned Indian boy was about to be killed by Indians upon whom his care would fall, generously took care of the child and sent him home to Mrs. Jackson to be raised with his son Andrew. Jackson was convinced that the barbaric state in which he encountered most Indians had

to change, but he was also convinced that the change was possible and to an extent inevitable if the Indians were to survive.

Much of Jackson's opinion about the status of the Indians was governed by his firm conviction that they did not constitute sovereign nations, who could be dealt with in formal treaties as though they were foreign powers. That the United States in fact did so, Jackson argued, was a historical fact which resulted from the feeble position of the new American government when it first faced the Indians during and immediately after the Revolution. To continue to deal with the Indians in this fashion, when the power of the United States no longer made it necessary, was to Jackson's mind absurd. It was high time, he said in 1820, to do away with the "farce of treating with Indian tribes." Jackson wanted Congress to legislate for the Indians as it did for white Americans.

From this view of the limited political status of the Indians within the territorial United States, Jackson derived two important corollaries. One denied that the Indians had absolute title to all the lands that they claimed. The United States, in justice, should allow the Indians ample lands for their support, but Jackson did not believe that they were entitled to more. He denied any right of domain and ridiculed the Indian claims to "tracts of country on which they have neither dwelt nor made improvements, merely because they have seen them from the mountain or passed them in the chase."

A second corollary of equal import was Jackson's opinion that the Indians could not establish independent enclaves (exercising full political sovereignty) within the United States or within any of the individual states. If their proper status was as subjects of the United States, then they should be obliged to submit to American laws. Jackson had reached this conclusion early in his career, but his classic statement appeared in his first annual message to Congress, at a time when the conflict between the Cherokees and the State of Georgia had reached crisis proportions. "If the General Government is not permitted to tolerate the erection of a confederate State within the territory of one of the members of this Union against her consent," he said, "much less could it allow a foreign and independent government to establish itself there." He announced that he had told the Indians that "their attempt to establish an independent government would not be countenanced by the Executive of the United States, and advised them to emigrate beyond the Mississippi or submit to the laws of those States." I have been unable to perceive any sufficient reason," Jackson affirmed, "why the Red man more than the white, may claim exemption from the municipal laws of the state within which they reside; and governed by that belief, I have so declared and so acted." . . .

Jackson was genuinely concerned for the well-being of the Indians and for their civilization. Although his critics would scoff at the idea of placing him on the roll of the humanitarians, his assertions—both public and private—add up to a consistent belief that the Indians were capable of accepting white civilization, the hope that they would eventually do so, and repeated efforts to take measures that would make the change possible and even speed it along.

His vision appears in the proclamation delivered to his victorious troops in April 1814, after the Battle of Horseshoe Bend on the Tallapoosa River. "The fiends of the Tallapoosa will no longer murder our Women and Children or disturb the quiet of our borders," he declared. "Their midnight flambeaux will no more illumine their Council house, or shine upon the victim of their infernal orgies. They have disappeared from the face of the Earth. In their places a new generation will arise who will know their duties better. The weapons of warefare will be exchanged for the utensils of husbandry; and the wilderness which now withers in sterility and seems to mourn the disolation which overspreads it, will blossom as the rose, and become the nursery of the arts."

The removal policy, begun long before Jackson's presidency but wholeheartedly adopted by him, was the culmination of these views. Jackson looked upon removal as a means of protecting the process of civilization, as well as of providing land for white settlers, security from foreign invasion, and a quieting of the clamors of Georgia against the federal government. This view is too pervasive in Jackson's thought to be dismissed as polite rationalization for avaricious white aggrandizement. His outlook was essentially Jeffersonian. Jackson envisaged the transition from a hunting society to a settled agricultural society, a process that would make it possible for the Indians to exist with a higher scale of living on less land, and which would make it possible for those who adopted white ways to be quietly absorbed into the white society. Those who wished to preserve their identity in Indian nations could do it only by withdrawing from the economic and political pressures exerted upon their enclaves by the dominant white settlers. West of the Mississippi they might move at their own pace toward civilization.

Evaluation of Jackson's policy must be made in the light of the feasible alternatives available to men of his time. The removal program cannot be judged simply as a land grab to satisfy the President's western and southern constituents. The Indian problem that Jackson faced was complex, and various solutions were proposed. There were, in fact, four possibilities.

First, the Indians could simply have been destroyed. They could have been killed in war, mercilessly hounded out of their settlements, or pushed west off the land by brute force, until they were destroyed by disease or starvation. It is not too harsh a judgment to say that this was implicitly, if not explicitly, the policy of many of the aggressive frontiersmen. But it was not the policy, implicit or explicit, of Jackson and the responsible government officials in his administration or of those preceding or following his. It would be easy to compile an anthology of statements of horror on the part of government officials toward any such approach to the solution of the Indian problem.

Second, the Indians could have been rapidly assimilated into white society. It is now clear that this was not a feasible solution. Indian culture has a viability that continually impresses anthropologists, and to become white men was not the goal of the Indians. But many important and learned men of the day thought that this was a possibility. Some were so sanguine as to hope that within one generation the Indians could be taught the white man's ways and that, once they learned them, they would automatically desire to turn to that sort of life. Thomas Jefferson never tired of telling the Indians of the advantages of farming over hunting, and the chief purpose of schools was to train the Indian children in white ways, thereby making them immediately absorbable into the dominant culture. This solution was at first the hope of humanitarians who had the interest of the Indians at heart, but little by little many came to agree with Jackson that this dream was not going to be fulfilled.

Third, if the Indians were not to be destroyed and if they could not be immediately assimilated, they might be protected in their own culture on their ancestral lands in the East—or, at least, on reasonably large remnants of those lands. They would then be enclaves within the white society and would be protected by their treaty agreements and by military force. This was the alternative demanded by the opponents of Jackson's removal bill—for example, the missionaries of the American Board of Commissioners for Foreign Missions. But this, too, was infeasible, given the political and military conditions of the United States at the time. The federal government could not have provided a standing army of sufficient strength to protect the enclaves of Indian territory from the encroachments of the whites. Jackson could not withstand Georgia's demands for the end of the *imperium in imperio* represented by the Cherokee Nation and its new constitution, not because of some inherent immorality on his part but because the political situation of America would not permit it.

The jurisdictional dispute cannot be easily dismissed. Were the Indian tribes independent nations? The question received its legal answer in John Marshall's decision in *Cherokee Nation* v. *Georgia,* in which the chief justice defined the Indian tribes as "dependent domestic nations." But aside from the juridical decision, were the Indians, in fact, independent, and could they have maintained their independence without the support— political and military—of the federal government? The answer, clearly, is no, as writers at the time pointed out. The federal government could have stood firm in defense of the Indian nations against Georgia, but this would have brought it into head-on collision with a state, which insisted that its sovereignty was being impinged upon by the Cherokees.

This was not a conflict that anyone in

the federal government wanted. President Monroe had been slow to give in to the demands of the Georgians. He had refused to be panicked into hasty action before he had considered all the possibilities. But eventually he became convinced that a stubborn resistance to the southern states would solve nothing, and from that point on he and his successors, John Quincy Adams and Jackson, sought to solve the problem by removing the cause. They wanted the Indians to be placed in some area where the problem of federal versus state jurisdiction would not arise, where the Indians could be granted land in fee simple by the federal government and not have to worry about what some state thought were its rights and prerogatives.

The fourth and final possibility, then, was removal. To Jackson this seemed the only answer. Since neither adequate protection nor quick assimilation of the Indians was possible, it seemed reasonable and necessary to move the Indians to some area where they would not be disturbed by federal-state jurisdictional disputes or by encroachments of white settlers, where they could develop on the road to civilization at their own pace, or, if they so desired, preserve their own culture.

To ease the removal process Jackson proposed what he repeatedly described as—and believed to be—*liberal* terms. He again and again urged the commissioners who made treaties to pay the Indians well for their lands, to make sure that the Indians understood that the government would pay the costs of removal and help them get established in their new homes, to make provision for the Indians to examine the lands in the West and to agree to accept them before they were allotted. When he read the treaty negotiated with the Chickasaws in 1832, he wrote to his old friend General John Coffee, one of the commissioners:

"I think it is a good one, and surely the religious enthusiasts, or those who have been weeping over the oppression of the Indians will not find fault with it for want of liberality or justice to the Indians." Typical of his views was his letter to Captain James Gadsden in 1829:

You may rest assured that I shall adhere to the just and humane policy towards the Indians which I have commenced. In this spirit I have recommended them to quit their possessions on this side of the Mississippi, and go to a country to the west where there is every probability that they will always be free from the mercenary influence of White men, and undisturbed by the local authority of the states: Under such circumstances the General Government can exercise a parental control over their interests and possibly perpetuate their race.

The idea of parental or paternal care was pervasive. Jackson told Congress in a special message in February 1832: "Being more and more convinced that the destiny of the Indians within the settled portion of the United States depends upon their entire and speedy migration to the country west of the Mississippi set apart for their permanent residence, I am anxious that all the arrangements necessary to the complete execution of the plan of removal and to the ultimate security and improvement of the Indians should be made without further delay." Once removal was accomplished, "there would then be no question of jurisdiction to prevent the Government from exercising such a general control over their affairs as may be essential to their interest and safety." . . .

Jackson's Indian policy occasioned great debate and great opposition during his administration. This is not to be wondered at. The "Indian problem" was a complicated and emotion-filled subject, and it called forth tremendous efforts on behalf of the Indians by some missionary groups and other humanitarians, who spoke loudly about Indian rights. The issue also became a party one.

The hue and cry raised against removal in Jackson's administration should not be misinterpreted. At the urging of the American Board of Commissioners for Foreign Missions, hundreds of church groups deluged Congress with memorials condemning the removal policy as a violation of Indian rights; and Jeremiah Evarts, the secretary of the Board, wrote a notable series of essays under the name "William Penn," which asserted that the original treaties must be maintained. It is not without interest that such opposition was centered in areas that were politically hostile to Jackson. There were equally sincere and humanitarian voices speaking out in support of removal, and they were supported by men such as Thomas L. McKenney, head of the Indian Office; William Clark, superintendent of Indian affairs at St. Louis; Lewis Cass, who had served on the frontier for eighteen years as governor of Michigan Territory; and the Baptist missionary Isaac McCoy—all men with long experience in Indian relations and deep sympathy for the Indians.

Jackson himself had no doubt that his policy was in the best interests of the Indians. "Toward this race of people I entertain the kindest feelings," he told the Senate in 1831, "and am not sensible that the views which I have taken of their true interests are less favorable to them than those which oppose their emigration to the West." The policy of rescuing the Indians from the evil effects of too-close contact with white civilization, so that in the end they too might become civilized, received a final benediction in Jackson's last message to the American people— his "Farewell Address" of March 4, 1837. "The States which had so long been retarded in their improvement by the Indian tribes residing in the midst of them are at length relieved from the evil," he said, "and this unhappy race—the original dwellers in our land—are now placed in a situation where we may well hope that they will share in the blessings of civilization and be saved from that degradation and destruction to which they were rapidly hastening while they remained in the States; and while the safety and comfort of our own citizens have been greatly promoted by their removal, the philanthropist will rejoice that the remnant of that ill-fated race has been at length placed beyond the reach of injury or oppression, and that the paternal care of the General Government will hereafter watch over them and protect them."

In assessing Jackson's Indian policy, historians must not listen too eagerly to Jackson's political opponents or to less-than-disinterested missionaries. Jackson's contemporary critics and the historians who have accepted their arguments have certainly been too harsh, if not, indeed, quite wrong.

A professor of history at the University of Wisconsin,
ROBERT F. BERKHOFER, JR. (b. 1931) is interested
in the interaction of cultures which occurred when
the Americans met the aboriginal Indians, and he
argues that the conflicts must be studied in the light
of the beliefs and cultural patterns of both sides at the
time. His *Salvation and the Savage* (1965) explores
the views of the Protestant missionaries, one of the
strongest groups working for the civilization and
assimilation of the Indians, in the period before the
Civil War. What were the objectives of the missionaries,
and why did these zealous men fail to achieve their
goals?*

Robert F. Berkhofer, Jr.

Protestant Indian Missions

Even the briefest outline of Protestant
missionary activity during the years
1787–1862 reveals enormous changes in
numbers of workers, scope of operation,
and fields of labor. At the end of the
American Revolution, only a dozen missionaries survived to carry the Gospel
to the perishing aborigines. These earlier
workers had been inspired by the Great
Awakening, but the large-scale operations
of the nineteenth century flowed from
that wave of pietism, called the Second
Great Awakening, which began in the
1790s and was responsible for so much of
the organized benevolence, particularly
Congregationalist and Presbyterian,
throughout the next century. After the
War of 1812, a nationalistic current joined

the wave of pietism to alter the course
of missionary history.

Inevitably the status of the new nation
compelled the societies organized from
the end of the Revolution to the War of
1812 to resemble the efforts of the colonial
period more than the future. The triple
lack of money, national outlook, and
cultural independence restricted the
size of the societies, the location of fields,
and experimentation with new methods.
Small budgets meant few missionaries
who had to serve in tribes close to society
headquarters. Difficulty of transportation
and communications as well as the triumph of state and regional bonds over
national loyalties reinforced this result.
All these factors determined that the

*From Robert F. Berkhofer, Jr., *Salvation and the Savage: An Analysis of Protestant Missions and Ameri-
can Indian Response, 1787–1862* (Lexington: The University of Kentucky Press, 1965), pp. 1–15, 152–160.
Footnotes omitted.

missionary work of this period be individual preaching and itineracy similar to colonial work.

The spirit of nationalism after the War of 1812 transformed the scope of missionary operations. Denominations organized churchwide societies which drew funds from members in all regions. Missionary directors envisioned stations strung across the continent, and an expanding economy and improved transportation made these dreams practical. More money meant larger stations staffed by missionaries who lived there year-round. Better transportation offered access to tribes farther away and enabled the missionary to serve the cause of Manifest Destiny.

Once part of national life, missionary operations were affected by national events. In the 1830s the federal policy of removing all the Indians to west of the Mississippi forced the relocation of most mission stations. Once relocated in the West, the missionaries directed their attention to Indians indigenous to the Indian territory as well as to regaining the confidence of their former eastern charges. At the same time, missionary societies expanded operations to the "wilder" savages of the Plains and even to the natives of the Pacific coast. In the next decade, the slavery issue began to hamper mission effort. The missionary current as part of the national tide broke upon the rocks of sectionalism. As denominations divided into northern and southern churches, missions were parceled out between the contending parties. Finally the turmoil of the Civil War compelled many mission stations to close their doors, and for that reason provides an appropriate terminal date for this study.

Yet for all these changes over time in staff, field, and size, the goal of Protestant missionaries and their patrons remained ever the same. In spite of denominational differences, there is striking similarity in the announcements of missionary aims.

Each newly founded missionary society professed as its main purpose the propagation of the Gospel. The first two societies founded after the Revolution expressed this aim in their titles—the Society for Propagating the Gospel among the Indians and Others in North America (1787) and the Society of the United Brethren for Propagating the Gospel among the Heathen (1787). The New York (1796), the Northern (1797), the Connecticut (1798), the Massachusetts (1799), and the Western Missionary Societies (1802) wrote such an aim into their constitutions—usually article two. In a later period both the American Board of Commissioners for Foreign Missions (1810) and the United Foreign Missionary Society (1817) proclaimed a like goal. The Baptists who drafted the preamble to the constitution of their society in 1814 hoped the organization would direct "the energies of the whole denomination in one sacred effort for sending the glad tidings of Salvation to the heathen, and to nations destitute of pure Gospel light." For the same reason the Missionary and Bible Society of the Methodist Episcopal Church in America (1820) desired to send missionaries and Bibles as "messengers of peace to gather in the lost sheep of the house of Israel."

This goal, as conceived by directors, missionaries, and their patrons, rested upon the basic Protestant tenet of the acceptance of the Bible as the sole standard of faith. To the Gospel was ascribed a miraculous power to produce conversion. But was no human agency necessary? In the missionary directors' opinion, all that was necessary in frontier *white* settlements destitute of religion was simply to collect funds sufficient to have Bibles printed, distributed, and expounded. But what was needed for the savage? The Word could be conveyed by preaching, but in that situation the listener relied partly upon the authority of the speaker. Should not the convert be able to determine matters of salvation for himself by reference to the Supreme Source as revealed in the Holy Scriptures? Was not literacy required, and did not this necessitate the founding of schools? Furthermore, did not the Indians need an economic system that would support the requisite schools and churches? In short, was not civilization as well as religion necessary to the establishment of scriptural self-propagating Christianity? As one writer said, "the Gospel, plain and simple as it is, and fitted by its nature for what it was designed to effect, requires an intellect above that of a savage to comprehend. Nor is it at all to the dishonor of our holy faith that such men must be taught a previous lesson, and first of all be instructed in the emollient arts of life."

Others replied that the miracle of the Word was enough and, in fact, only through prior acceptance of the Truth and its reforming virtues could the savages be elevated to civilization. Persons who claimed otherwise supported the atheistic doctrine that a means more powerful than the Gospel miracle was available. The Word was the means of God, and conversion was not by human agency but by the Holy Spirit—"it is the *power of God* to salvation." One minister thus advised the infant New York Missionary Society: "Instead of waiting till Civilization fit our Indian neighbors for the gospel, let us try whether the gospel will not be the most successful means of civilizing them. . . . One Christian institution

alone, the holy sabbath, will go farther to civilize them in a year, than all human expedients in a century."

Thus the issue was joined, and the debate over whether first to civilize or to Christianize the savage raged throughout the pre-Civil War period. Denominations, on the whole, took different sides of the question, but regardless of position, neither side ever precluded either the spread of Christianity or civilization to the exclusion of the other. Rather the argument over the method of propagating the Gospel was reduced to a simple precedence of procedure in the dissemination of two desirable objects. Furthermore, in the actual operations of various societies, civilization and Christianity were inextricably combined. Thus the problem was really more one of semantics than of actual difference, and the real question becomes: What meaning did the words "civilization" and "Christianity" possess in the minds of missionaries and their supporters in the seventy-five years under review that inevitably made them link the two concepts together?

Civilization as conceived by Americans in this period meant an upward unilinear development of human society with the United States near the pinnacle. Comprising civilization was a cluster of institutional arrangements that Americans sought to achieve between the Revolution and the Civil War. Economically, they moved toward allowing economic individualism free rein under the liberal state. Politically, they first realized republicanism, then democracy. Lastly, the liberty of the individual was foremost in their minds; hence all social institutions were assumed to exist solely for the benefit of the individual (white) members of society. Ethnocentric Americans believed that the idea of progress pointed toward a future modeled upon their way of life; thus their manifest destiny, if not mission, was to spread their superior institutions into the western wilderness and even beyond their country's boundaries.

To the missionaries as to most Americans, Protestantism was an inextricable component of the whole idea of civilization. Quite explicit was the thinking of Stephen Riggs, the famous Sioux missionary, who wrote in 1846: *"As tribes and nations the Indians must perish and live only as men!* With this impression of the tendency of God's purposes as they are being developed year after year, I would labor to prepare them to fall in with *Christian civilization* that is destined to cover the earth."* In another instance, a committee on Indian missions reported to the Baptist Board director in 1822 that it "anticipated a period not far distant when the Indian shall be brought not merely to unite with the white men in the worship of God, but cooperate with them in the business of Agriculture and Trade." Therefore, it advised the board to work toward self-sustaining Indian settlements "where the refinements of civilized society shall be enjoyed" and to work among red men yet savage so as "to carry the gospel and the blessings of civilized life to the dark and distant regions of the west, until the rocky mountains shall resound with harmony and praise and the shores of the Pacific shall be the only boundary of this wide sweep of human civilization and Christian benevolence." . . .

Because missionaries and their patrons dealt with alien cultures, many of them saw what few people generally see—the functional interrelationship of the various institutions in a society. Thus they saw, in a sense, that they spread what is called today an integrated cultural system, an entire blueprint for living which struc-tured institutions and the roles individuals played in them. In the most sophisticated statement of missionary purpose written during the period, the American Board of Commissioners for Foreign Missions recognized this situation: "Missions are instituted for the spread of scriptural self-propagating Christianity. This is their only aim. Civilization, as an end, they never attempt; still they are the most successful of all civilizing agencies, because (1) a certain degree of general improvement is in a self-propagating Christianity, and must be fathered as a *means* thereto; and (2) a rapid change in the intellectual and social life is a sure out-growth therefrom." It was for this reason that missionaries found themselves, as one confessed, "entirely unable to separate religion and civilization," and the version of their culture which they propagated may be called, as some of them termed it, "Christian civilization." Therefore, the only good Indian was a carbon copy of a *good* white man, or as a Methodist missionary wrote, "In the school and in the field, as well as in the kitchen, our aim was to teach the Indians to live like white people." . . .

Not only did the missionaries' concept of civilization set their goals, but it also explained the object of their benevolence. That the early nineteenth-century Americans could not observe the Indian without measuring him against their own society has been amply demonstrated by Roy Harvey Pearce in his book, *The Savages of America.* A certain type of cultural relativity and moral absolutism combined in this view to show that though white and red man were of the same biological mold, the Indian possessed customs that fitted him perfectly to his level of development in the history of man, but the level was far inferior to that of the white European. The savage was the zero point of human society. As Pearce remarks, "Savage life and civilized life are realms apart, separated by centuries of cultural history, or by entirely different environmental situations, most likely by both." Thus even seemingly superior savage traits were products of an inferior society and, though excellent for this level, were backward in a more advanced society. Men of the period evaluated not so much the qualities of individual Indians but those of a society by placing it in relation to their own in such a way that the idea of progress solved the problem of evaluation. The idea of history as progress made it possible for them to comprehend the other culture as earlier, hence morally inferior. Therefore, seemingly objective observations on Indian character were always normative analyses of what the Indian should be in terms of nineteenth-century American society. Thus were the aborigines accounted uncivilized.

Persons engaged in the missionary movement particularly viewed the objects of their benevolence in this manner, because moral evaluation was their stock in trade. Pearce uses the Moravian missionary John Heckewelder and Jedidiah Morse, who not only was influential in missionary circles but shaped many Americans' views of the Indians by his writings, as illustrations of his thesis. Even missionaries sympathetic to the Indian described him as if he were a negative prototype of all that was civilized. For instance, in the middle of the nineteenth century, a Baptist missionary could write after years of contact with his flock:

Very indefinite, not to say erroneous, ideas prevail respecting the character and condition of the Indians. . . . The milder affections are active, especially in their domestic relations, and their hospitality to strangers is prover-

bial. Parental love is strong to a fault, and the death of a child is not infrequently the occasion of extreme agony, though proportionally brief. . . . Their cruelty to persons of war results more from errors in their moral code than from a cultural thirst for blood.

They have some marked peculiarities:— they are naturally, or from habit, indisposed to regular industry, impatient of restraint, fickle, prodigal, and reckless. The fiercer passions, envy, jealousy, anger, malice, by no means lack occasions of development; and without the restraint of higher principles than their reason and the light of nature afford, sometimes rage to a fearful degree. In the conjugal relation they have special need of the gospel to strengthen and hallow the marriage bond.

The directors of the missionary societies may not have held such enlightened views. An article in one religious magazine noted, "the condition of the heathen is truly deplorable. Their minds are in gross darkness. They know not the True God nor the only Savior of lost sinners; and are strangers to that blessed gospel which 'has brought life and immortality to light.' They are exceedingly depraved, and enslaved to sin, Satan, and the world."

In light of these attitudes, missionaries and their supporters believed both Indian institutions and Indian "character" had to be transformed. The necessary institutions were those already possessed by Americans. As a Presbyterian missionary remarked, "It is to make these [savage] abodes of ignorance and degradation, as happy, as gladsome, as the happiest and most gladsome village in our peaceful land." The arrogant savage was to be turned into a man of humility who implicitly believed, "Industry is good, honesty is essential, punctuality is important, sobriety essential." This new man also abhorred idleness and considered labor good for the body and "not unprofitable to the spirit." The Christian Indian was to manifest "tenderness of conscience, a docility, and a desire for further instruction" in the great mysteries. Yet many missionaries wanted him also to show "Yankee enterprise—go ahead determination."

What was the method required to achieve these goals of character transformation and civilized institutions? Fieldwork was to be a simple matter of instruction to be accomplished quickly— if all men were rational. Not thinking in terms of cultures as is done today, but in terms of "human nature," the missionaries and their patrons assumed the same system of basic values was held by savage and civilized alike. If a savage merely lacked knowledge of the more advanced condition to which human society had evolved, then a missionary had but to point out the way and the savage would adopt it. Any right-thinking savage should be able to recognize the superiority of Christian civilization when shown him. Thus in regard to secular knowledge, the New York Missionary Society directors instructed their missionary among the Tuscaroras to "persuade" the Indians "by every rational motive to the practice of civilization, and to relish the enjoyments of domestic society" by pointing out to them that the whites increased in population because they farmed. "This argument will operate on the feelings of the patriotic Indian, and will serve to establish with convictive energy the arguments adduced from self interest, so clearly evinced in the diminution of bodily fatigue, in the alleviation of mental anxiety, & improvements of domestic comforts; [and] will strengthen [and] confirm the more powerful [and] weighty motives derived from the obligations of Religion." Likewise with Christianity, since Protestantism embraced the highest evolution of morals, the missionary had

only to mention its superiority over savage degradation to secure mass conversion. Thus, not only were the goals of mission societies prescribed by the sponsoring civilization, which was only to be expected, but even the method used to achieve these aims developed in line with a preconceived image of the Indian rather than through field experience.

Since conversion to Christ and civilization was conceived as an instructional problem, mission stations were educational establishments in the broadest sense. There the Indians would be persuaded by "right reason" and rationally calculated self-interest to adopt the white religion and ways, and would learn how to pray, farm, and behave. Whether the stations were large model communities in the form of manual labor boarding schools or small model families as represented by a missionary couple, all stations served three functions—piety, learning, and industry—and were to model school, church, home, and farm. Only a detailed examination of these efforts in terms of the missionary mentality will persuade the reader how no custom was too picayune for censure and change, and no demand too sweeping and drastic in the missionaries' attempts to revamp aboriginal life in conformity with American ideals. . . .

* * *

The "white fields," according to the religious magazines of the period, beckoned the Lord's workers to reap the bountiful harvest of converts. Nineteenth-century faithful were certain Christ's second coming was imminent, and in preparation for this glorious event, the Lord commanded the rapid mass conversion of heathen all over the world—for nothing less would satisfy the Lord or his optimistic nineteenth-century agents.

Yet this optimism was not borne out by the statistics reported from the field. After thousands of dollars and hundreds of missionaries, the managers and patrons of the missionary societies had to account their eight decades of effort among the American Indians as unsuccessful. Although the modern analyst can see only the inevitable failure of the missionary enterprise given the participants' cultural assumptions in the contact situation, the religious observers of the time never saw clearly the extent of their failure or the reasons why the Lord's promise remained unfulfilled.

From the very beginning, missionary groups reached opposite conclusions, based upon the same facts, about the success or failure of their efforts. The preacher who delivered the annual discourse in 1808 to the Boston Society for Propagating the Gospel considered the colonial efforts to Christianize the aborigines successful and pointed to John Eliot, the Mayhews, Bournes, and Sergeants, as well as Wheelock, Brainerd, Hawley, and Kirkland as proof that "other men before us have labored in this work with success." His colleague who presented the first address to the society viewed the efforts of these men in quite another light but hoped for better results in the future: "Although the attempts to Christianize the Indians of North America, hitherto have been attended with little effect, it is the wish of the pious and benevolent that attempts may be still continued. If experience has pointed out defects and errors, in former attempts, new experiments, and conducted on different principles, may hereafter succeed."

The rush to new methods and new experiments reached its zenith in the years following the War of 1812. In the first flush of enthusiasm and under the millennial hopes of mass conversion,

society after society eagerly reported their experiments to be crowned with success. The United Foreign Missionary Society happily proclaimed in 1823: "that the American Savage is capable of being both civilized and Christianized, can no longer be questioned. The problem is already solved. Successful experiment has placed the subject beyond doubt."

Yet the very continuance of protests that the Indians could embrace Christian civilization revealed it as doubtful in the minds of many. In 1852 both the American Baptist Missionary Union and the American Board of Commissioners for Foreign Missions assured its supporters that the practicability of Indian work was demonstrated by the progress of their missions. The Baptist Committee declared how under missionary exertions "thousands of these tribes, who once roamed through the forests in quest of a precarious subsistence, have been reduced and won over to habits of sober and regular industry; cultivating the soil with the skill of Christian civilization, and depending on its products for a more sure support. And what is of infinitely greater account, many of these have been brought to know, to love, and to obey the Savior, and to enjoy the hope of the regenerate child of God." The American Board took inventory of its missionary operations after thirty-five years and pointed with pride to its Cherokee, Seneca, and Tuscarora missions, but singled out for special praise the Choctaw mission. Its missionaries in that tribe ministered to 1,300 church members, which added to the same number cared for by other denominations equaled about one-eighth of the total population. The Choctaws had renounced drunkenness and adopted and followed a law of total abstinence. They had abandoned the chase to pursue farming. In addition they boasted of a good educational system, a written constitution, and decent government. So like their white neighbors were these Indians, asserted an aged missionary, that "the man who marries and does not provide a house and farm for his family, is in as poor repute among the Choctaws, as he would be among the whites."

In spite of such optimistic reports, however, only one society ever voluntarily closed any of its missions with the claim that its work was legitimately accomplished. The American Board discontinued its Tuscarora and Cherokee missions in 1860. For well over sixty years various societies had labored among the Tuscaroras. As early as 1804 the New York Missionary Society had concluded that the tribe was well on its way to civilization and Christianity. Yet efforts were continued, and a half century later the missionary to the tribe maintained that his charges could be counted among the civilized and Christian nations of the earth and, in fact, were more temperate, more proper in Sabbath observance, less profane, and more respectful of religion than their white New York neighbors. He boasted that a third of the Tuscaroras were church members. . . .

In reality, the American Board probably closed these two missions more for financial reasons than from any deep conviction about the success of their labors. No other society followed the board's example among the Cherokee Tribe or any other tribe. Why after all their praying, preaching, and plowing did the missionaries and their patrons not consider their efforts in achieving their goal of self-propagating Christianity fruitful enough to warrant discontinuing their missions?

To the missionary mind of the period, the experiment to civilize and Christianize the American aborigines was bound to be interpreted as a failure. The criteria for judging the experiment's success were part of the basic value system of the culture in which the judges lived. Yet the very social assumptions that determined the goals hindered their realization, for these assumptions failed to correspond with the cultural reality of the contact situation. Hopes were raised of a quick success impossible in light of the cultural theory of today and unobtainable with the methods available to the missionary of that period. To complicate the judging further, the evaluation of the Indians' achievements was always in comparison with a variety of American culture that differed from observer to observer according to class, religion, and other subcultural variation, so that no general agreement ever resulted. From these difficulties stem the various contemporary opinions upon the outcome of missionary work in the period between the Revolution and the Civil War—and even after.

Thus the advance of Indian Christianity was both hailed and depreciated. Even so simple a thing as whether the observer preferred a religion stressing strong doctrinal knowledge or more emphasis upon emotional fervor determined the outcome of the analysis, for it was easier for the Indians to display the latter than to learn the former. Or, the more exclusive a religion the observer considered Christianity, the more he searched for and condemned syncretistic practices, and the fewer Christians he could find. Baptists, for example, judged success in quite different terms than did Congregationalists. Even if the Indians achieved the religious conditions of the white population—as the missionaries reported the Tuscaroras and Cherokees had—many observers did not concede success, for they condemned the American nation as merely nominally

Christian and not fully converted. Therefore, these men actually demanded more of the Indian tribes but recently missionized than was found in their own society which was a part of the Christian heritage. Most tribes never reached this level, but missionization was slowly proceeding. However, missionaries and their patrons desired and expected rapid mass conversion because of their assumptions of a universal human nature and the attendant lack of a concept of culture. For that reason they accounted this slow success a failure.

Since the observers favored a self-propagating Christianity among the aborigines which depended upon their assuming *implicitly* an inextricable linkage between religion and civilization, the tribes had to develop the same social institutions as the whites in order to sustain sufficiently religion in the eyes of the missionaries and their patrons. Yet the more time consumed in teaching the Indians to plow and wash, the less time for prayer and catechism. By trying to provide a civilized foundation for Christ's Church, the missionaries lost the goal in the attempt to gain it. On the other hand, not to teach civilization meant the Indians would never achieve a basis for a self-sustaining religion and so the mission could never be closed. This dilemma only existed because the missionary mind *explicitly* divorced the elements of culture, unlike the theorists of today. In reality, civilization and Christianity had to go hand-in-hand, and this explains the slow progress of missionization. Furthermore, at the same time the missionaries were bringing a variety of American civilization into the forests, that civilization at home was rapidly changing in technological aspects. While this did not alter the missionary approach to the transformation of Indian character and life,

it could not help but widen in white minds the gap between white and Indian ways. Even if the Indians had achieved the material condition the whites possessed at the commencement of missionization, the Indians would still have been considered backward in light of the subsequent change in American civilization. Here success turned bitter because the goal had actually changed.

The failure to see success was not the only cause for the lack of success in the missionaries' eyes. True, the missionaries could not account their work fully fruitful because of the peculiar framework of social assumptions that sustained their efforts, but objective cultural reality contributed to the failure to achieve their goals. Certainly as significant as the missionary outlook in making success difficult was the unanticipated consequences of success—factionalism. Whether the missionary created a division in the tribe or was thrust onto an existing side upon entrance, the presence of factionalism removed a significant part of the village or tribe from his influence. The greater the success of the missionary, the sharper the division and the less his influence over the other side. If the factions adopted different denominations, then the missionization succeeded, but in such a case religion was duly subordinated to other interests against the missionaries' hopes and protests.

Even the faction favoring Christian civilization could not reach the ideal envisaged by the missionaries and their supporters, not because of the Indians' desire to retain old customs but because of American racial attitudes. To realize the ideal fully, the Indians should have become integrated into the larger white society. In many cases the failure of the aborigines to achieve this goal of Christian civilization was due to civilized Christians not accepting them on equal terms, for American society traditionally discriminated against non-Caucasian peoples. By discriminating against the aborigine upon the basis of a belief of white cultural superiority, Americans forced the Indian to remain savage and guaranteed the failure of the missionary program. American citizenship, which symbolized this aim, was withheld not only because of Indian unwillingness but because of white intolerance. In some ways this discrimination caused the Indian to attempt to revive his demoralized traditional culture.

On the other hand, the anticivilization faction deliberately clung to the old ways. Even under the strong impact of American civilization, the old patterns persisted though externals and material objects had changed. This faction stubbornly resisted the missionaries even though to fight them and the other forces of the dominant society, they borrowed elements from the culture they fought in order to resist it more effectively.

The laborers in the Lord's vineyard were doomed not to reap the harvest they hoped because of their own cultural assumptions, the racial attitudes of their compatriots, and the persistence of aboriginal culture. For these reasons the missionaries could both praise their efforts in light of the growth of church rolls and yet condemn them in light of their hopes. The increasing discouragement of the missionary directors and their public with Indian work in spite of the agonizingly slow growth of Indian Christianity during the period was reflected in the annual reports of the various societies. Less and less space was devoted to American Indian missions, and mention of them was shifted further back in the report as missionary directors and patrons saw millennial hopes dashed upon the stubborn reality of culture conflict and misunderstanding.

Uncle Sam's Stepchildren by LORING BENSON
PRIEST (b. 1909), published in 1942, is still the best
treatment of the post-Civil War efforts to assimilate
the Indians into the mainstream of American life. In
the first sections of the book Priest describes early
reform efforts and traces the destruction of the treaty
system and tribal autonomy. In the final section, from
which the following selections are taken, he provides
a perceptive account of the formulation of the policy
that looked toward citizenship for the Indians and
distribution of their lands in severalty. He ends with
a critical evaluation of the Dawes Act (1887), which
was the culmination of the Indian reform movement
of the period. Is his appraisal after fifty years a
convincing one?*

Loring Benson Priest

The Dawes Act and Indian Reform

While the portions of the Dawes Act
dealing with the problem of Indian citizenship were of the utmost importance,
the primary purpose of the measure was
to revolutionize the method of Indian
land holding. The age-old practice of
communal or tribal ownership was to be
ended by dividing reservations into plots
for distribution to individual Indians.
The race would advance more rapidly,
reformers held, if each Indian was encouraged by receiving personal title to
the land he occupied. As a measure limited to abandoning communal for several
ownership would not benefit the whites,
however, more than a mere change in the
method of land holding was necessary to
win the favor of legislators. The Dawes

Act was accepted by Congress only after
its sponsors had made strange compromises between plans intended to aid the
Indian and those meant to annex his land.

Two land holding provisions of the
Dawes Act reveal unusually well the way
in which Indian and white interests were
balanced. Considerations of Indian welfare were uppermost when legislators
provided that allotments should not be
sold for twenty-five years. Yet self-interest
was just as obviously the motive when
Congress insisted that all unallotted land
should immediately be opened to white
settlement. Although funds from the sale
of excess land were to be used for benefit
of the Indians, the fact remained that
undisputed title to a definite portion of

*From Loring Benson Priest, *Uncle Sam's Stepchildren: The Reformation of United States Indian Policy,
1865–1887* (New Brunswick, N.J.: Rutgers University Press, 1942), pp. 217–220, 227–232, 250–252. Footnotes
omitted.

85

land was to be gained only by surrender- ing any claim to the rest. Whether such a policy would prove of benefit to whites, to Indians, to both races, or to neither was far from certain.

The significance of the debates regard- ing land policy can be comprehended much more clearly after a brief summary of the arrangement which was ultimately approved. The process was to begin when- ever the President believed that the mem- bers of a tribe would benefit from land distribution. An affirmative decision having been reached regarding the ad- visability of allotment, each head of a family was to receive one-quarter section (160 acres), each single person over eigh- teen as well as each orphan child was to have one-eighth section (80 acres), and all other single persons under eighteen born prior to an allotment order were to be assigned one-sixteenth section (40 acres). Where insufficient land existed, *pro rata* assignments were to be made in the same proportion; and where reser- vations were only of use for grazing, the amounts were to be doubled. In no case, however, was full title to an allotment to be granted for twenty-five years. In- dians were to be prevented from dispos- ing of their holdings during this time by patents declaring that the land was held in trust by the United States for the exclusive use of the allottee and his heirs. If still further protection proved desirable at the end of the period, government con- trol might be extended indefinitely at presidential discretion. Once the patents had been issued to each Indian, or sooner if felt desirable by the President, unal- lotted areas were to be sold to white set- tlers. Sums realized from the disposal of such land were to be deposited in the United States Treasury and the annual interest accumulated by the funds was to be employed for the education and civi-

lization of the tribe. Thus stated, the prin- ciples of the Dawes Act seem extremely simple. In reality, the system was pieced together only after extended debate as to what plan would aid whites the most while injuring Indians the least. Land provisions of the Dawes Act were not exclusively a product of sympathy for the Indian.

In stating that many supporters of the Dawes Act were moved by selfish motives, the impression should not be created that self-seeking legislators were from any particular part of the country. Motives were often so mixed even in the case of individual congressmen that no section's attitude can be characterized as either exclusively selfish or unselfish. The de- sire of frontiersmen to dispossess Indians was naturally strong; but interest in secur- ing land was a powerful factor in winning the support of men from all sections. A conviction that no Indian land should be "a barrier against the swelling tide of American commerce" was universal. Rep- resentatives of frontier states were more apt than their colleagues to emphasize the advantage of severalty legislation to whites, but arguments of Easterners ex- plaining the gains to be made by Indians were almost always accompanied by oth- ers urging the neccessity for commercial expansion. As Easterners had every rea- son to be more liberal, their emphasis upon the desirability of obtaining more Indian land was especially significant.

The interest of frontiersmen in opening Indian reservations to settlement was shared by both the individual reformers and the organizations of the East. Few Easterners believed that Indians should occupy land they could not use. Even a woman, who held that Indians as "Dece- dents of Father Abraham" were "within the covenant of mercy," wrote President Grant that if red men felt they had a right to their lands "it was high time they were better inform'd." Undeniable as were the rights possessed by Indians, Senator Dawes believed that the advance of white civilization was as impossible to check as a river. Members of the Indian Rights Association not only agreed, but announced that they would not resist a legitimate advance of civilization if they could. So eager was their Washington representative to open reservations that he declared the purpose of filling the Indian Territory with settlers "ought never to sleep." Similar interest in expansion led the Mohonk conference of 1884 to hail passage of a bill redistributing Sioux land as much because of the opening of a new highway as for any advantage gained by the Indians. Even members of the Board of Indian Commissioners, who were particularly noted for their concern for the Indian, refused to uphold his land claims. Instead, they ably summarized the opinion of a large majority of Americans by writing in their 1879 *Report:*

We may moralize over the natural rights of the Indian as much as we please, but after all they have their limit. His right to the soil is only possessory. He has no title in fee. If he will cultivate it and use it as civilized men use their possessions, it will or should be well with him, but it is evident that no 12,000,000 acres of the public domain, whose hills are full of ores, and whose valleys are waiting for diligent hands to "dress and keep them," in obedience to the divine command, can long be kept simply as a park, in which wild beasts are hunted by wilder men. This Anglo-Saxon race will not allow the car of civilization to stop long at any line of latitude or longitude on our broad domain. If the Indian in his wildness plants himself on the track, he must inevitably be crushed by it.

The white man's passion for possession was too great to protect Indian rights from invasion even by those known for their sympathy with the oppressed. . . .

The nature of the compromise which enabled passage of the land provisions of the Dawes Act has already been described. No measure could have been successful without provision for the sale of large portions of the reservations. Yet reformers were strong enough to insist that no Indian land should be taken without compensation. As a result, the sale of surplus land was balanced by granting a secure title to the remainder and setting aside all profits to be used for racial advancement. Whether or not such a policy would prove fair to the Indians and whether or not it could be successfully administered remained to be discovered. But as far as most contemporaries were concerned, a plan for remodeling Indian policy had been found which would prove equally advantageous to the members of both races.

The forced sale of surplus land was naturally the most popular administrative provision of the Dawes Act. As early as 1870, Quakers had officially proposed that superfluous Indian land should be sold to secure money for education and the establishment of tribal members upon individual allotments. Since many students of Indian affairs believed advancement would be impossible as long as tribes were permitted to roam over large areas, plans for reducing reservations by the sale of land received wide support and were occasionally adopted for restricted use. Government officials were not enthusiastic about applying the idea generally as they realized the difficulty of securing a satisfactory administration of land sales and tribal funds. Westerners likewise opposed plans for the acquisition of surplus land as long as hope remained that Indians might be completely removed from a reservation instead of being presented with a clear title to any portion of it. But as the impossibility of further removals became apparent, frontiersmen displayed an increasing willingness to grant land to individual Indians in return for admission to areas which were not needed. Enthusiasm for such an arrangement mounted irresistibly when legislators proposed that claims for damages pending against a tribe should be paid from funds obtained from sale of its land! Even though reformers insisted that money derived from land sales should be used exclusively for purposes of civilization, frontiersmen hoped to divert purchase money into the hands of border communities so that the land of the Indians might be secured without expense. This purpose was ultimately defeated; but in the meantime Western support insured success for the proposal to sell surplus land. Action was delayed until 1887 only because details had to be worked out which would facilitate administration and provide adequate compensation for the Indians.

Problems to be decided before the sale of surplus land could be successfully instituted were far more complicated than the apparent simplicity of the process would indicate. Success or failure might well depend upon whether allotments were selected by the Indians or by government administrators. Yet the superiority of neither method was clear. If complete freedom of choice was permitted, unintelligent selections could not be prevented and land necessary for commercial expansion might be absorbed. But if plots were assigned by the government, Indian antagonism would be aroused and opportunity provided for the intrigues of selfish officials. Even though a decision might be avoided on this controversial point, the question remained whether

allotments should be compact or scattered throughout a reservation. While Senator Teller of Colorado was so convinced of the need for racial contact that he endeavored to limit severalty assignments to alternate quarter sections, most legislators wished to confine Indian settlements within as restricted an area as possible. Thus all plans for mixing the races were thwarted in spite of Senator Dawes's interest in encouraging contact; and gaps in assignments were not even permitted either for communal use or to supply the future needs of a tribe. Decisions of equal importance also had to be reached concerning the funds obtained from land sales. Congress debated at length whether every cent should be made available for tribal use at presidential discretion. Senator Dawes was willing to allow the executive department to control the entire fund, but fellow senators successfully insisted that only the interest might be spent without specific congressional authorization. While such problems were only a few of those which arose during discussion of the sale of surplus land, agreement regarding the Dawes Act was even more seriously delayed by the necessity of deciding what protection should be offered Indian allottees.

The portion of the severalty act which made Indian allotments inalienable for twenty-five years was adopted in spite of violent protests against withholding any areas from prospective buyers. Although the speed with which red men had lost their land under early allotment measures emphasized the importance of prohibiting the sale of all land assigned to Indians, a powerful group fought every effort to protect the race. Yet no doubt regarding the validity of such inalienation provisions was possible in the light of Supreme Court decisions. When purchasers endeavored to retain land sold by a Kansas Indian without government consent, the justices refused the claim and discouraged further suits by declaring:

It was considered by Congress to be necessary, in case the reservees should be desirous of relinquishing their occupation of their lands, that some method of disposing of them should be adopted which would be a safeguard against their own improvidence; and the power of Congress to impose a restriction on the right of alienation, in order to accomplish this object, cannot be questioned. Without this power, it is easy to see, there would be no way of preventing the Indians from being wronged in contracts for the sale of their lands, and the history of our country affords abundant proof that it is at all times difficult, by the most careful legislation, to protect their interests against the superior capacity and adroitness of their more civilized neighbors.

In cases where Congress failed to forbid sale, the Court subsequently held that Indians might dispose of their title even before a patent had been issued. But the Court made clear that whenever Congress banned alienation of Indian allotments such restrictions were entirely legal.

Although the legality of prohibitions against the sale of Indian land could not be questioned, many Americans refused to admit the justice of providing Indian land holders with special protection. If red men were sufficiently advanced to be granted citizenship, opponents of inalienation insisted that they should be required to take care of themselves. True freedom would be impossible, they pointed out, as long as Indians were prevented from disposing of their allotments. In most cases, this hatred of inalienation was due to hope of obtaining land from Indian owners. Yet some friends of the race also criticized prohibitions against the sale of allotments on the ground that Indian independence should not be jeopardized

in any way. Ill-considered insistence that red men must stand upon their own feet was evident, for example, in the remarks of a Baptist reformer who declared:

The land belongs to them or it does not. If it does belong to them, give it to them; but we give it to them as I give anything to my little son. I say, "That is yours, but don't you sell it, my boy." Well then it is *not* his. The Indians are simply playing that it is theirs, while we have everything in our power to do as we please.... The time is coming when we should step forth and recognize the rights of these Indians to citizenship and property. If they lose their property, they are doing no more than we have done before them. More than one-half of us are losing ours, but we go to work and get more ... "Root hog or die" is a principle; and let us put them in a position to "root."

Fortunately such an extreme view of the necessity for independence was exceptional among reformers. Most leaders of the Indian movement were too well informed to disregard the fact that allotment measures must prove ineffective unless provisions were included protecting Indian titles.

Inclusion of an inalienation provision in the Dawes Act did much to counteract portions of the bill which were less favorable to the Indians. Yet some reformers considered the twenty-five year prohibition inadequate even after a clause had been added allowing an indefinite extension of the period by presidential action. Senator Miller of California believed that Indians would not be ready to forego United States protection in less than fifty years. But even if government control had been made perpetual, officials rarely displayed sufficient interest in protecting Indian land to justify confidence that any prohibition against sale would be of value. In many cases, the United States had been unnecessarily slow in issuing patents.

Puyallup Indians were forced to wait thirty years because their land was desired by the Northern Pacific; while delay in granting inalienable patents to the Crows led their disgruntled agent to expose the folly of inconsistent Washington land administration by writing:

It would be better to maintain the reservations *forever* (reducing them to reasonable size) than to patent lands to Indians without making them inalienable.

The government is altogether too slow in these matters.

It is too slow in doing what is right, and after going slow for a few years it wakes up and litterally *"makes a break"* and then is too fast in doing what is wrong (as for instance in patenting lands to Indians in Kansas and other places without making them inalienable).

It is provided by treaty with these Indians—the Crows—that their homesteads shall be inalienable, and there is no reason in this world why with this proviso every patent should have been issued by this date . . . The only reason it has not been done is that the people at Washington dont know anything about this work.

It sometimes seems as if they were incapable of learning or else that they dont care.

Whatever protection was provided at the moment, the safety of the Indians depended upon future legislators and administrators. The very fact that many Americans wished to force severalty upon the Indians regardless of treaty obligations raised the question whether inalienation clauses might not be similarly abrogated if Congress so desired. Yet as long as people feared that Indians would become paupers and vagabonds if freed from government control, special protection was certain to be widely advocated. Even if the effectiveness of inalienation provisions had been indisputable, however, there would still have been reason to question whether the increased protection was worth the price demanded.

In attempting to determine whether the Dawes Act adequately defended Indian interests, the aims of its supporters must be distinguished from its results. The measure would certainly never have been adopted if its provisions had been considered exceptionally unjust to the Indians. Too many Americans were interested in Indian welfare at the time to permit acceptance of plans intended to destroy the race. But advocates of the Dawes Act did not deny that Indians would lose land. Pressure upon reservations was so strong that a realistic outlook forced recognition of the necessity for surrender of some Indian land in return for an undisputed title to the rest. If legislators could have insured that secure title to good land would be granted, encouragement of individual initiative by limitation of Indian holdings might have proved possible. Since the success of the compromise depended upon future administration, criticisms of the measure were justified.

Like many other Indian measures, the Dawes Act failed to achieve a just balance between white and tribal interests. In 1880 General Armstrong had complained, "The Indian question has been put wrong end first. It points to us not to them." A similar criticism could have been made of the Severalty Act of 1887. Most friends of the measure were more interested in securing Indian land than in establishing a just policy for the control of Indian affairs. Contemporary critics were able to point out that if legislators were really interested in Indian advancement they might teach them to use their land instead of taking it from them on the ground of idleness. As funds obtained from the sale of Indian land would only tend to strengthen racial indolence, some commentators announced that the red men would be "better off with the land than the proceeds." Certainly national progress did not have to be made at the expense of the Indians. Reformers who feared that allotment would prove a means for robbing the tribes were much more realistic than those who held that whites would respect the property of industrious Indians. With Senator Dawes hesitating to push the measure for fear that the Indians *would* not receive good land, and with evidence existing that many settlers were determined that Indians *should* not receive good land, Bland wisely suggested that the reform should at first be limited to experiments undertaken on a small scale among advanced tribes, and that in even these instances the sale of surplus land should be postponed until a more adequate idea of the amount of land needed by the Indians was obtained. But instead of agreeing to apply the severalty program gradually, impatient legislators exerted every effort to speed application of the new policy. . . .

In judging the Dawes Act half a century after its passage, no one can deny that the expectations of its sponsors were never realized. Senator Dawes himself confessed only a few years after the Act had passed that the measure would never have been placed on the statute books if the radical character of the resulting changes had been realized. As his daughter testified in later years, Dawes expected aid from churches, philanthropic societies and advanced Indians which never materialized. Lacking such assistance, President Cleveland and Secretary Lamar were frequently unable to resist pressure for immediate allotment. Their less cautious Republican successors not only refused to struggle against the tide, but boasted that Secretary of the Interior Noble had "opened to settlement more Indian reservations than all of his predecessors combined." With administrators anxious to seize Indian land as rapidly as possible, Dawes was soon forced to complain that only an eye witness could understand how vain and cruel the policy of forcing was proving. Before half a decade had passed, United States officials had clearly demonstrated that they were either unable or unwilling to use the Dawes Act for Indian benefit.

No important changes were made in the Dawes Act for several years in spite of the abuses which immediately appeared. Reformers who believed the administration of the Act rather than its principles at fault, finally succeeded in securing fundamental modifications in the Burke acts of 1906. Thus the right of citizenship was withdrawn from allottees because of the number of incompetent tribes granted land in severalty, and the inalienation period was extended because few Indians showed any indication of ability to meet white competition despite years of individual land holding. Such moves were the result of serious dissatisfaction with administration of the Dawes Act. Until the presidency of Franklin Roosevelt, however, there was little suggestion that land allotment itself was undesirable. Yet today the Act, which was compared by contemporaries with Magna Charta and the Declaration of Independence, is officially regarded as merely the latest and most contemptible feature of America's long abuse of the Indian race.

A study of the background of the Dawes Act cannot close without a brief appraisal of the contemporary Indian policy of the United States. Although allotment was the outgrowth of a desire for expansion, it was also the product of a sincere conviction that emulation of the whites was essential. In prohibiting individual ownership of land, Washington officials of the present day must confess either that Indians cannot or that they should not live like other citizens. The current Indian program clearly abandons all effort to establish individual independence. Some change was necessary, one must admit, as previous attempts to make a place for the Indian in American society had failed. Whether an absolute reversal was wise is another question, for failure to pursue one goal persistently has always been a major fault of American Indian policy. It is unfortunate, for instance, that under the current program Indians who have shown their ability to adapt themselves to modern conditions are faced with the unenviable choice of returning to tribal life or breaking from their race. If individual ownership of land could be made compatible with racial preservation by careful government administration, the excesses of both past and present might be avoided. If not, the return to a policy of isolation will mean the defeat of fifty years of effort to solve the Indian problem. In either case, modern sympathy for the Indian must prove more lasting than that of the eighties if future Indian policy is to escape the pitfalls of indifference.

In spite of the failure of the Dawes Act, the sponsors of Indian reform in the years following the Civil War deserve praise for their work. The first attempt to solve the problem permanently was the most significant step taken to aid the red man since the formation of the Republic. Superficial efforts at reform proving insufficient, a small group undertook the introduction of vital changes. By organization and pressure combined with clever compromises, success was finally achieved and the old, out-moded system replaced by a new. Unfortunately these Indian workers, as reformers both before and since, viewed their plans too optimistically, and pushed rapidly ahead without realizing that caution was desirable or that even citizenship itself might prove disastrous. Subsequent generations may well wish the advance had been less hasty; yet they can hardly regret that for the first time in the history of the country sympathy for the Indian received concrete expression. Like most measures, the Dawes Act was a mixture of selfishness and idealism. But although self-seeking was not absent, legislators made the measure memorable by providing a definite plan for the Indian's future. The failure resulting was unfortunate; but misapplication by administrators rather than the evil intent of legislators was responsible for the disastrous history of America's first systematic effort to provide for Indian welfare.

From 1933 to 1945 JOHN COLLIER (1884–1968) served
as United States Commissioner of Indian Affairs. A
social reformer with deep sympathy for Indian culture,
he became the architect of a "New Deal" for the
Indians, which reversed the long attempt to force the
Indians into the white man's patterns of culture. In the
following selections from his book *Indians of the
Americas* (1947), Collier sets forth the principles upon
which his Indian reform was based and describes the
legislative enactments that embodied them. How did
his reforms overturn the principles of the Dawes Act?*

John Collier

The Indian New Deal

In March, 1933, Franklin D. Roosevelt
entered into office as President of the
United States. Harold L. Ickes became
the new Secretary of the Interior. I was
appointed the new Indian Commissioner.

I had been learning a great deal about
the American Indian himself, and about
other men and women who knew the Indian, for over twelve years; and my staff
and I, always with the firm support of
Harold L. Ickes and the active and personal interest of the President, formulated
a set of principles that have remained
dominant. They may be summarized this
way:

First, Indian societies must and can be
discovered in their continuing existence,
or regenerated, or set into being *de novo*
and made use of. This procedure serves
equally the purposes of those who believe
the ancient Indian ways to be best and
those who believe in rapid acculturation
to the higher rather than the lower levels
of white life.

Second, the Indian societies, whether
ancient, regenerated or created anew,
must be given status, responsibility and
power.

Third, the land, held, used and cher-
ished in the way the particular Indian
group desires, is fundamental in any life-
saving program.

Fourth, each and all of the freedoms
should be extended to Indians, and in the
most convincing and dramatic manner
possible. In practice this included repeal

*From *Indians of the Americas* by John Collier. Copyright, 1947, by John Collier. Reprinted by arrangement with The New American Library, Inc., New York. Pp. 154–159, 169–171. Footnote omitted.

of sundry espionage statutes, guarantee of the right to organize, and proclamation and enforcement of cultural liberty, religious liberty, and unimpeded relationships of the generations.

Fifth, the grant of freedom must be more, however, than a remission of enslavements. Free for what? Organization is necessary to freedom: help toward organizing must be extended by the government. Credit is necessary to freedom: cooperatively managed credit must be supplied. Knowledge is necessary to freedom: education in terms of live local issues and problems must be supplied through activity programs in the schools; technological and business and civic education must be supplied to adults; professional and collegiate training must be opened to the post-adolescent group. Responsibility is necessary to freedom: one responsibility is perpetuation of the natural resources, and conservation must be made mandatory on the tribes, by statute. Capital goods are necessary to freedom, and responsibility must be applied to capital goods: a tribe that handles its revolving credit fund irresponsibly must know that shrunken credit will be its lot tomorrow.

And now, the sixth principle: The experience of responsible democracy, is, of all experiences, the most therapeutic, the most disciplinary, the most dynamogenic and the most productive of efficiency. In this one affirmation we, the workers who knew so well the diversity of the Indian situation and its incalcitrancy toward monistic programs, were prepared to be unreserved, absolute, even at the risk of blunders and of turmoil. We tried to extend to the tribes a self-governing self-determination without any limit beyond the need to advance by stages to the goal. Congress let us go only part way, but the part way, when admin-

istrative will was undeviating, proved to be enough. Often the administrative will was not undeviating, often the administrative resourcefulness was not enough, often the Gulliver's threads of the land allotment system and of civil service and the appropriation systems kept the administrator imprisoned. The establishment of living democracy, profound democracy, is a high art; it is the ultimate challenge to the administrator. The Indian Service since 1933 has practiced the art, has met the challenge, in ways varied enough and amid situations diversified enough to enable one to give a verdict which seems genuinely momentous: the democratic way has been proved to be enormously the efficient way, the genius-releasing and the nutritive and life-impelling way, and *the way of order.*

The seventh principle I would call the first and the last: That research and then more research is essential to the program, that in the ethnic field research can be made a tool of action essential to all the other tools, indeed, that it ought to be the master tool. But we had in mind a particular kind of research impelled from central areas of needed action. Since action is by nature not only specialized but also integrative of specialties, and nearly always integrative of more than the specialties, our needed research must be of the integrative sort. Again, since the findings of the research must be carried into effect by the administrator and the layman, and must be criticized by them through their experience, the administrator and the layman must themselves participate creatively in the research, impelled as it is from their own area of need. Through such integrative research, in 1933, the Soil Conservation Service directly originated in the ecological and economic problems of the Navajo Indian tribe. In current years integrative research (the administrator and layman always participating) has pushed far back our horizons of knowledge and understanding of a whole series of the tribes, and has searched our policies, administration, personnel and operating methods to their foundations. I add, in passing, that such research invariably has operated to deepen our realization of the potentialities of the democratic way, as well as our realization of our own extreme, pathetic shortcomings.

In 1934 the Indian Reorganization bill was laid before Congress, where the hearings on it lasted several months. Some people ridiculed this bill because it contained 52 printed pages. They forgot that it was offered as a successor to the greater part of several thousand pages of Indian law. Until 1934, Indian tribes rarely had been consulted on the legislation introduced for their supposed benefit. In preparing this bill, however, the Indian office first sent to all the tribes questions concerning the Indian problems deemed to be central. Then the bill was furnished them all. Finally, congresses of Indians were held in all the regions, gatherings in which practically every tribe in the United States was represented.

As originally introduced in Congress the bill had six main parts.

1. The Indian societies were to be recognized, and be empowered and helped to undertake political, administrative and economic self-government.

2. Provision was made for an Indian civil service and for the training of Indians in administration, the professions and other vocations.

3. Land allotment was to be stopped, and the revestment of Indians with land was provided for.

4. A system of agricultural and industrial credit was to be established, and the needed funds authorized.

5. Civil and criminal law enforcement, below the level reached by federal court jurisdiction, was to be set up under a system of courts operating with simplified procedures and ultimately responsible to the tribes.

6. The consolidation of fractionalized allotted lands, and the delivery of allotments back into the tribal estate, was provided for under conditions which safeguarded all individual property rights and freedoms.

The first four parts of the Reorganization bill, as listed, became law. The fifth and sixth parts were lost. The fifth part may have been fortunately lost, because the tribes, under the enacted parts of the bill and under court decisions defining the unextinguished, inherent powers of Indian tribes, are coping with law and order more effectively with each passing year. But the loss of the sixth part was a major disaster to the Indians, the Indian service and the program. Congress has not yet righted that blunder of 1934. The fractionalizing of allotted Indian lands rushes on; the real estate operation of leasing these atomized parcels and collecting and accounting for and paying out the hundreds of thousands of vanishing incomes becomes increasingly costly, and increasingly a barrier against productive work or thinking in the allotted jurisdictions; millions of their best acres remain unusable to the Indians.

In the meantime, however, the Indian Service and the tribes are struggling to reverse the flood that is eating away the Indians' land-base. This is being done through voluntary exchanges and relinquishments, which require contact with each of the all but innumerable heirs — fifty heirship equities may vest in one Indian, and one allotment may have hundreds of scattered heirs. Despite the difficulties, the wasting flood has been checked and reversed in a few jurisdictions. It is only where this occurs that there can be a beginning of the positive program of using Indian lands through Indian effort. The situation was fully recognized in the report of the House Subcommittee on Indian Investigation, issued in December, 1944. In passing so lightly over this very important subject I wish only to add that in this matter, too, the Indians are wrestling with a problem widely encountered in other lands. One of the heavy drags on the agricultural economy of Asiatic India, for example, is the ever-increasing fractionalization of farm holdings. The formulae that are being successfully used here in the United States (but far too gradually, in the absence of the Congressional authority sought but not obtained) have application in Europe and in Asia.

The Reorganization bill, as finally enacted, contained a requirement that every tribe should accept or reject it in a referendum held by secret ballot. Those who accepted the act could organize under it for local self-government. Through a subsequent referendum they could organize themselves as federal corporations chartered for economic enterprise. Ultimately, about three-fourths of the Indians of the United States and Alaska came within the act. A related enactment, the Johnson-O'Malley Act, also passed in 1934, provided for the devolution of federal power to states and other political subdivisions, and for the enlistment of private agencies in the Indian task, through a flexible system of contracts and of grants-in-aid.

The Indian Service, on the basis of this legislation and impelled by the principles enumerated above, has striven to the end that every one of the particular programs —conservation, the cattle program, community organization, schools, the credit program, health, the Indian branch of the Civilian Conservation Corps and the

other depression-years programs, the arts and crafts work—that every particular program should serve the primary aims of freeing or regenerating the Indian societies, and infusing them with the spirit of democracy, implementing them with democratic tools, and concentrating their attention upon their basic practical exigencies. Year after year, and cumulatively with the years, we who were doing the work observed sadly our partial failures, here and there our complete failures. Yet we also witnessed a development that has far outweighed the deficiences.

We have seen the Indian prove himself to be the best credit risk in the United States: of more than $10,300,000 loaned across ten years, only $69,000 is today delinquent. We have seen the Indian beef-cattle holdings (nearly always they are managed co-operatively) increase 105 per cent in number of animals and 2,300 per cent in yield of animal products; and we have seen this increase take place on ranges that in varying measures were gutted by erosion caused by overgrazing twelve years ago, and now, in general, are overgrazed and gutted no more. We have watched scores of ancient tribal systems reorient themselves toward modern tasks, while more than a hundred tribal democracies have been newly born and have lived and marched out into life; these democracies are political, industrial and social. We have witnessed the Indian peoples giving themselves with ardor and discipline to the war; 25,000 of their young people have served in the armed forces, with the highest volunteering record, we believe, of any population in the country. Finally, we have seen the Indian death rate more than cut in half, and for this achievement the expanded and improved clinical services supply only a partial explanation: the changed anticipation, from death to life, the world winds that blow at last within what were the reservation compounds, the happiness and excitement of democratic striving and clashing and living—this is the significant explanation of a 55 per cent decrease in the death rate in less than ten years. . . .

The policies established by legislation in 1934 have withstood every attack, except the attack through appropriations. Increasingly in recent years the appropriations acts of Congress have been made vehicles of covert legislation. The appropriations sub-committees, especially in the House of Representatives, are all but autonomous; the House gives only a fiction of deliberative consideration to the annual supply bills. In numberless cases Congress has concluded after careful deliberation that such and such policies shall be law, and has then proceeded to rubber-stamp appropriation bills which nullify and reverse the policies.

Specifically, in the Indian field, land acquisition for Indians, authorized by Congress, is blocked through the appropriation bills; the situation is similar with respect to the expansion of the Indian co-operative credit system. Congress legislated that Indian tribes and corporations should be given technical advice and assistance in their operations, and then the appropriation act nullified the legislation. The United States entered into treaty with thirteen other Western Hemisphere countries, and by the treaty pledged herself to maintain a National Indian Institute; the House subcommittee on Interior Department appropriations has flaunted the treaty commitment. In general, the appropriation acts have handicapped the Indian Service and the Indians in the realization of every democratic, libertarian policy that Congress has established as the law of the land.

This anomaly of our Congressional system has effects, of course, far beyond Indians and dependencies and ethnic problems. Precisely because it is an evil of so universal a reach, we may expect it to be corrected in times ahead. While it lasts, it hangs like a gloomy shadow over the Indians and over territories and dependencies such as Alaska, the Virgin Islands and Puerto Rico.

From the Indian record we can draw these conclusions:

First, biological racehood, whether it exists or not, is without practical importance. There accumulate within and around races that are biologically distinguishable, and within and around races that are not biologically distinguishable, those in-group and out-group factors whose aggregate is called "racial." The factors are socially caused and socially transmitted.

Second, in ethnic matters, as in other vital matters, governmental intervention can be baneful or benign. In any field of human relations, when government tries to do the whole job, authoritatively and monopolistically, the result is baneful. The earlier Indian record is replete with evidence of this. But when government makes research an inseparable part of its ethnic operations, eschews monopoly, acts as a catalytic and co-ordinating agent, offers its service through grants-in-aid to local subdivisions, then government can be decisively benign, as the recent Indian record demonstrates. It is of national importance, and necessary to the good role of our Occidental governments in the world, that ethnic groups shall have equality of opportunity, shall be enabled to contribute their ideals and genius to the common task, shall not suffer discriminations, shall be free to breathe deeply the breath of public life. The Bill of Rights and the Constitution within the United States, the Charter of United Nations in the world, must be made good. It follows that governments and the federation of governments should and must concern themselves with ethnic matters, and that the methods should be right and not wrong.

Third, the individual fares best when he is a member of a group faring best. All human beings, in young childhood at least, are members of groups. The group is the tree and they are the fruit it bears. At least up to a certain age-level, the individual reft from his group is hurt or destroyed. The ruin inflicted on Red Indians through the white man's denial of their grouphood, and his leading them to deny their own grouphood, is only a special case of something that is universal. It may be that contemporary white life is being injured nearly as much by the submergence of its primary social groupings as the denial of Indian grouphood injured Indian life. If the primary social group in white life were regenerated for full functioning, through resourceful and sustained social effort, and were dynamically connected once more with the great society, the hygienic and creative results might be no less startling than those observed in the comeback of Indian societies.

Fourth, in ethnic groups of low prestige the apparent inferiority (acquired or innate) may mask an actual superiority. In most Indian groups the academic lag of children is pronounced, but if these children were given non-language tests that have been standardized on whites, they excel, even to a sensational extent. Their elder brothers excel when they are thrown into critical action, as they have been in the recent world war. In rhythm, so little regarded in our white society, the Indians excel. In public spirit they excel, and in joy of life, and in intensity realized within quietude. They excel in art propensities, and in truthfulness. These superiorities will be masked by an apparent inferiority until their group as a group moves into status and power. Then the mask will fall away. The application of this fact to underprivileged ethnic groups in general is readily apparent.

And last, the Indians and their societies disclose that social heritage is far more perduring than is commonly believed. On how small a life-base, on a diminished and starved life-base for how many generations, the motivations and expectations of a society, and its world-view and value system and loyalties, can keep themselves alive; how these social possessions, which are of the soul, can endure, like the roots and seeds on the Mojave desert, through long ages, without one social rain; and how they rush, like these roots and seeds, into surprising and wonderful blossom when the social rain does come at last. Perhaps no other ethnic groups have revealed this old, all-important truth so convincingly as the Indians have done. Indeed, this capacity for perdurance is one of the truths on which the hope of our world rests—our world grown so pallid in the last century, and now so deathly pallid, through the totalitarian horror. The sunken stream can flow again, the ravaged desert can bloom, the great past is not killed. The Indian experience tells us this.

The goal of most Americans in dealing with the Indians has been to assimilate the natives into the dominant white society. Yet after centuries of contact the Indian cultures persist with an amazing strength. EVON Z. VOGT (b. 1918), professor of anthropology at Harvard University, explores this phenomenon in the article printed here. He briefly describes the historical fact and, on the basis of numerous recent studies, suggests possible explanations. He leans toward the view that in the United States acculturation has been hindered by "persisting Anglo-American 'racial' attitudes," inflexible attitudes that devaluate other cultural traditions.*

Evon Z. Vogt

Acculturation of American Indians

By the mid-twentieth century it has become apparent to social scientists studying the American Indian that the Indian population of the United States is markedly increasing and that the rate of basic acculturation to white American ways of life is incredibly slower than our earlier assumptions led us to believe. During the latter part of the nineteenth century and the early part of this century, the American Indians were prevailingly thought of in American public opinion as a "vanishing race." Vestiges of this opinion are, indeed, still with us as illustrated by the fact that an impressive "Memorial to the American Indian" is shortly to be built on the outskirts of Gallup, New Mexico—at the edge of the Navaho Indian country where the Navaho population has increased from 15,000 (at most) in 1868 to almost 80,000 in 1956 and where Navaho culture persists with great vigor!

We were led to these comfortable assumptions about the vanishing American Indian by the fact that there *were* important population declines earlier in our history—many Indian tribes, in fact, became extinct—and by the observation that the Indians *had* undergone impressive changes in certain aspects of their cultures. It was anticipated that the population decline would continue and that the acculturative changes would proceed apace with all tribes and in all aspects of their culture as white American institu-

*Evon Z. Vogt, "The Acculturation of American Indians," *The Annals of the American Academy of Political and Social Science*, vol. 311 (May, 1957), 137–146. Footnotes omitted.

tions impinged upon them. Earlier generations of young anthropology students were urged to go into the field and collect ethnographic data on Indian culture before it completely disappeared.

It has also been felt strongly that just as European immigrant groups are becoming Americanized within a few generations in the great American "melting pot" so, too, will the American Indians become assimilated. However, students did not stop to raise seriously enough the question of the vast difference between the American Indian and the Europeans. European immigrants all came from the same general stream of Western culture and they, by and large, were motivated toward assimilation when they migrated to the United States. Not only were the Indians linguistically and culturally completely different from the peoples of Europe, but they also had little choice in the matter. European culture came to them in their native habitat and proceeded by force to overrun the continent.

The acculturative changes which formed the basis for our earlier observations involved several different kinds of processes. These processes have been in operation in varying degrees since 1540 when Coronado arrived at Zuni and established the first contact between Europeans and American Indians within what are now the continental borders of the United States. In the first place there has been an important "drifting out" process from almost all American Indian populations over the centuries in which individuals and families have left their native settlements to take up residence in American communities. In some cases, this rate of migration has been great enough to involve almost all of the Indian population; but in many other cases, it has had the effect of "draining off" the most acculturated segment of the population each

generation and of leaving a conservative reservoir of more traditional culture carriers intact to carry on their Indian way of life. We now also perceive clearly that we must differentiate between acculturative changes taking place in these individuals and families that are drifting away from the traditional ways of life and the Indian sociocultural system which may be undergoing quite a different type of change and at a much slower rate. This difference between *individual* change and *system* change in acculturation situations is fundamental, and it means that we should not jump to the conclusion that full acculturation will soon take place simply because we observe a certain segment of the population leaving Indian country to take up residence in the white world.

A second widespread and continuing process has been the replacement of Indian material culture with goods, techniques, and technological equipment of the white American way of life. There is no American Indian tribe today who is living close to the aboriginal level in its patterns of food, clothing, and shelter. But it is now clear that just because Zuni Indians, for example, build more modern type houses with running water and electric lights, invest in radios and refrigerators, and drive new automobiles, it does not mean that they necessarily abandon their kinship obligations or give up dancing in Katchina dances. Indeed, it has been startling to many of us to observe how completely the inventories of material culture in Indian households are composed of items derived from white American culture, and, yet, how relatively slow the rate of change is in social organization and religion in the same community.

All American Indian populations have also been undergoing a process of increasing involvement with our white American sociocultural system: in economic relationships to our market economy; in crucial adjustments to our state and national political systems, which now hold the ultimate control of force, and to our educational system, which now provides schools for almost all Indian children; in important connections with Christian missionary movements that now touch every Indian population. The earlier isolation of Indian populations from the main streams of modern life has decreased markedly in the past few decades, and today only one tribe—the Havasupai living deep in a branch of the Grand Canyon in northern Arizona—cannot be reached by automobile. As a result, the languages, social structures, and religions have all shown some change as the modern world closes in upon the Indian cultures.

But what is interesting to the close observer is that, despite all these pressures for change, there are still basically Indian systems of social structure and culture persisting with variable vigor within conservative nuclei of American Indian populations. It would be rash indeed to predict now that these cultural features will completely disappear in the course of acculturation in one, two, or even several generations.

This proposition raises the fundamental question as to why we have had to alter our earlier expectations concerning the rate of American Indian acculturation and why full acculturation to white American ways of life is not occurring in the contemporary scene. In this article I shall outline a conceptual framework for the analysis of American Indian acculturation, provide a brief synoptic review of the acculturation situation in different areas of the United States, and then discuss the limiting factors to full acculturation by comparing the situation of the United States with that in Mexico. The final section will consider the development of "Pan-Indianism" as an emerging stage in American Indian acculturation.

Conceptual Framework for the Analysis of Acculturation

Although students of American Indian acculturation are not yet ready to provide a definitive synthesis of the processes, we have developed a framework for understanding the general outlines in terms of two sets of variables: (a) *the nature of the two cultures which come into contact,* involving such questions as the types of sociocultural integration, settlement pattern, attitudes toward strangers, and so forth, and the intercultural compatibility of these patterns; and (b) *the contact conditions,* involving such questions as whether the contact is "forced" or "permissive," of long or short duration, intensive or sporadic, and so forth. The interaction between these two sets of variables leads to the types of intercultural relationships we observe and to a complex and varied set of processes of change that are just beginning to be understood adequately. These processes are of two major orders which may be differentiated by the terms "microscopic" and "macroscopic." The microscopic comprise specific recurring sequences of events in acculturation, such as the diffusion of concrete objects between the two cultures—the replacement of stone by steel axes being a classic example of this type of process. The macroscopic comprise the more pervasive patterns of change which persist over long-time spans and involve alterations in the sociocultural systems. In the first case the results have more to do with simple additions, subtractions, or replacements in cultural and linguistic *content;* in the second instance the results have more to do with *structural* and *pattern* changes, of which we are able to identify a number of different types— "additive," "fusional," "isolative," "nativistic," "assimilative," and so forth.

Synoptic Review of the Acculturation Situation

. . . My purpose here is merely to outline certain of the major trends in acculturation in terms of the two sets of variables we utilize to account for the processes.

East of the Mississippi

By and large, the Indian populations were forcibly removed from the areas east of the Mississippi River as the American population expanded and the frontier moved West. It is significant that the conditions of contact were such that it did not make much difference as to whether the aboriginal cultures were loosely integrated, scattered small bands of Northeastern Algonquian peoples or more complexly organized agricultural peoples such as the Southeastern Cherokee, Creek, Choctaw, and Chickasaw. By about 1845 the removal was substantially completed, and today only scattered small pockets of Indian population remain, principally in isolated regions—the Eastern Cherokee in the Great Smoky Mountains of North Carolina; the Seminoles, a subdivision of the Creek, who found refuge in the everglades in Florida; six small clusters of Iroquois in New York State and the Oneida who moved to Wisconsin in 1832; several groups of Algonquian peoples in the northern woods of Michigan, Wisconsin, and Minnesota; and a few other remnants such as the Abnaki in Maine.

But, even in this region, where the pressures for acculturation have been maximal, certain basic Indian cultural patterns persist with surprising vigor. This has been recently demonstrated by the work of Speck and Broom on the Cherokee; Spoeher and Sturtevant on the Seminole; Fenton, Wallace, and others on the Iroquois; and Keesing, Hallowell, Spindler, and others on the Algonquian peoples.

The Plains

In the prairie and plains between the Mississippi and the Rocky Mountains, removal took place later and was not carried to the same extremes. Oklahoma on the Southern Plains was utilized as a region in which to resettle many of the displaced Eastern tribes and a large number of the Prairie and Plains tribes. In the Dakotas and eastern Montana a number of large Indian populations, especially the Dakota, or Sioux, remain on reservations. Other small remnants include the Mesquakie, or Fox, in Iowa, and the Omaha and Ponca in Nebraska.

The removal or reduction of the Plains tribes involved a great deal of violence in the latter half of the nineteenth century. The development of strong warfare patterns and the use of the horse and gun made these tribes into formidable opponents for the United States Army. The Indian wars which took place on the Plains have so impressed themselves on the national consciousness as to make the Plains Indian into the prevailing stereotype of the American Indian. It is also significant that some of the most important nativistic reactions to occur in the United States came in the wake of these developments on the Plains—the Ghost Dance, followed by the less nativistic, more traditional Peyote Cult.

Again, although pressures for acculturation throughout this area have been great and the acculturation which has occurred has involved much personal frustration and demoralization for individual Indians, certain basic Indian ways of life persist in almost all cases, even in such apparently highly acculturated groups as the Mesquakies near Tama, Iowa.

Intermontane Region

It is certainly no geographic accident that all the large remaining Indian populations of the United States are located west of the 20-inch rainfall line. Here the land is much less desirable for farming without irrigation, and the total population density continues to present a marked contrast to that of the more humid eastern half of the nation. An additional important historical dimension was added to this picture by the fact that the main frontier of white settlement leaped across the arid intermontane region in the mid-nineteenth century when gold was discovered on the Pacific coast. These facts had special significance for the Southwest which I shall discuss below, but they were also important in lessening the pressures for early and forced acculturation in the territory to the north.

Through much of the intermontane region, especially in the Great Basin of Utah and Nevada, the aboriginal cultures were at such a low level of technological development and sociocultural integration as to create a contact situation in which these Shoshonean peoples had little to lose and much to gain by attaching themselves by small kinship units to the scattered ranches and mining camps. In this situation acculturation has proceeded quite rapidly and with relatively little strain.

Pacific Coast

In the Pacific coast region strong acculturative forces were set in motion by the middle of the nineteenth century after gold was discovered in California

and desirable lands were made available for settlement in Oregon and Washington. White-American population increased rapidly, and the Indian cultures were not organized to withstand much pressure. The result was the complete extinction of many groups and the reduction of others to small remnant populations living, in most cases, on reservations made up of a number of different Indian cultures. The Warm Springs reservation in Oregon with a combination of Wascos, Sahaptins, and Paiutes is a good example. In these cases Indian cultural patterns have not completely disappeared, but the process of acculturation has moved much further than it has in the Southwest, for example, and within a much shorter time period.

The Southwest

There is not much doubt that we find the largest and most conservative nuclei of American Indian populations in the Southwest. Here the time span of European contact has extended over four centuries, but the earlier Spanish control did not effectively reach the scattered encampments of the Apachean tribes, nor penetrate effectively to such tribes as the River and Upland Yumans. The major efforts were directed toward the Eastern Pueblo; the Hopi villages were never brought under effective control and the Zuni villages only periodically. The Pueblos were characterized by a relatively high degree of sociocultural integration in aboriginal times. The major effect of the Spanish effort seems to have been to add a few material culture items—such as wheat, domestic livestock, and a veneer of Catholicism—but it also increased the effectiveness of their boundary-maintaining mechanisms which operated against further acculturation in social organization and religion.

Since gold was discovered in California

right after the United States acquired this territory, the American frontier also tended to leap across the Southwest, leaving the Indian lands and cultures intact for an additional generation. Effective Anglo-American control did not come until late in the nineteenth century, following the roundup of the Apachean tribes and the coming of the railroad. Only in the past fifty years have contact conditions been such as to lead to new trends in acculturation. As of 1956, the acculturation situation is changing fast; but at the same time, Indian populations are increasing throughout the Southwest, and conservative nuclei of most tribes will certainly maintain Indian patterns for many generations to come.

Limiting Factors to Full Acculturation

A number of hypotheses have been advanced to account for the persistence of Indian culture in the face of increasing pressure from white American society toward full acculturation and the complete assimilation of Indian populations. To mention only a few of the common hypotheses, there is, in the first place, the argument, often advanced by the lay public, that isolation of the Indian populations on remote reservations administered by the Indian Bureau has insulated them from proper exposure to educational facilities, mass communications, and so forth and has prevented them from obtaining the means for assimilation. This hypothesis had undoubted merit, but it certainly fails to account for the many cases of Indian groups which have been subjected to a great deal of contact, yet who continue to maintain many of their old patterns. Witness, for example, the Tuscarora living on the outskirts of Niagara Falls, New York, or

the Isleta Pueblo located within fifteen miles of Albuquerque, New Mexico.

A more interesting hypothesis, also emphasizing contact conditions, has been advanced by Dozier and others to the effect that "forced" acculturation, if not so extreme as to lead to early absorption of the subordinate group, will result in a high degree of resistance to change in indigenous cultural patterns. This formulation appears to work well for cases like the Southwestern Pueblo where the aboriginal sociocultural systems were highly enough organized to develop patterns of resistance when "forced" acculturation occurred. It applies less well to tribes with a low level of aboriginal sociocultural integration, and, of course, does not apply at all to cases where the acculturation process was relatively "permissive" and the groups still maintain their old patterns.

A third type of hypothesis, involving a theory about the nature of culture, has been the thesis that while the material aspects of a culture can change readily, family and kinship institutions are more persistent; that the aspects of a way of life which have been labeled as core culture, implicit values, cultural orientations, and personality type, are still more persistent. This type of hypothesis appears to apply to certain tribes and to some ranges of our data. But the formulation in its present form will not account for all the variability we observe in rates of change in different aspects of American Indian culture. It also does not answer the basic question as to why *any* Indian patterns should be preserved at all considering the kind and degree of pressure for change many Indian tribes have experienced.

Still a fourth hypothesis stresses the importance of an organized communal structure. Eric Wolf has recently characterized this structure as a "corporate" community that maintains a bounded social system with clear-cut limits, in relation to both outsiders and insiders, and has structural identity over time. His thesis is that in Latin America the persistence of Indian-culture content seems to have depended primarily on maintenance of this structure and that where the structure collapsed, traditional cultural forms quickly gave way. This formulation has not been systematically explored with United States–Indian data; but it strikes me as an attractive hypothesis, especially in accounting for the high degree of persistence we observe among still very conservative tribes living in compact communities, like the Southwestern Pueblos. It is also crucial in explaining many of the differences between the acculturation of the American Negroes and the slower acculturation of the American Indians. But what concerns us more in this attempt to understand the limiting factors to full acculturation is why some important Indian patterns continue to persist among groups whose corporate structure has been shattered.

In all of these hypotheses, and others which cannot be discussed for lack of space, it is my impression that we have tended to de-emphasize recently, in our analyses of United States–Indian data, what is perhaps the most important factor of all: our persisting Anglo-American "racial" attitudes, derived historically from Puritan Colonialism, which strongly devaluate other physical types bearing different cultural traditions. These inflexible attitudes are of course directly related to the superordinate-subordinate structural character of Indian-white relationships in the United States. They are also related to the lack of a large mixed Indian-white population which would provide cultural models and reference groups along the continuum of acculturation for the conservative nuclei still living in the native-oriented Indian communities.

We pay lip service to the idea of Indians being the "First Americans," we now manifest considerable interest in their customs, and we decorate our homes with Indian rugs and pottery and dress our women in fashionable "squaw dresses" derived from Indian styles; but the barriers to full acceptance measured by such an index as the rate of intermarriage are still formidable in most areas of the United States. There are, of course, exceptions in some localities, as among the Menominee of Wisconsin, among the Wascos on the Warm Springs reservation in Oregon, or in parts of Oklahoma where intermarriage is more frequent. There has also undoubtedly been some admixture in all areas over the centuries. But taking the nation as a whole and considering especially the localities of high Indian population, such as the Southwest, the rate of miscegenation with whites continues to be astonishingly low.

The contrast with Mexico is sharp and illuminating. In Mexico interbreeding between Spanish and Indian began almost immediately after the Spanish conquest. Even though miscegenation was prohibited during the late Colonial period, the total process has moved far enough to produce a profoundly "mestizo" nation. There are still relatively unacculturated and unassimilated Indians remaining in various parts of the nation; but when Indian groups enter a transitional stage and begin to move in the direction of integration, there are cultural models and reference groups for them all along the continuum of acculturation, from the most native-oriented Indian communities to the sophisticated urban life in Mexico City. The sociocultural system is also open for the ambitious and talented Indian individual like Benito Juarez who began his career in an isolated Zapotec Indian village and went on to become one of Mexico's greatest presidents. But, even more important, the system is relatively open for transitional Indian groups as they proceed generation by generation along the continuum to fuller integration and acculturation. There is now a conscious and conspicuous positive valuation of the Indian heritage on the part of Mexico's political and intellectual leaders.

In the United States, on the other hand, the path to full acculturation is confusing and frustrating, and an ultimate ceiling is still firmly clamped down by our persisting Anglo-American "racial" attitudes. Instead of proceeding generation by generation along a continuum to full acculturation, it is as if an American-Indian group must at some point leap across a spark gap to achieve a fully integrated position in white American society.

I do not mean to imply that biological interbreeding per se affects the process, but that biological miscegenation leads to profoundly different self-conceptions and evaluations; to the kinds of reference groups that seem to provide a kind of natural "ladder of acculturation" in many areas of Mexico that is so conspicuously lacking in the United States; and to a much more permeable barrier at the extreme end of the acculturation continuum.

Pan-Indianism

Since a kind of ultimate lid or ceiling has been placed upon full acculturation and assimilation in the United States, it is now pertinent to raise the question as to what is happening to Indian groups who become reasonably well educated by our standards and move a great distance from their aboriginal ways of life without becoming fully integrated in the larger United States society. One way of looking at the problem is that we shall continue with a type of cultural pluralism for some generations to come. But in a vast number of cases, the process has moved too far for Indian groups to continue to find much meaning in their own particular aboriginal cultures, and what appears to be emerging is an interesting type of "Pan-Indianism."

This Pan-Indianism is assuming a form in which increasing numbers of American Indians are participating in customs and institutions that are describable only as Indian. These customs and institutions are being synthesized from elements derived from diverse Indian cultures and to some extent from white American culture. There exists also in many regions, and especially in Oklahoma, a loosely knit, informally organized grouping of Indians who have joined forces to participate in these Pan-Indian activities.

Historically, the beginnings of this type of Pan-Indianism are found in many of the nativistic movements which followed in the wake of conquest, the spread of the Ghost Dances being a classic type of example. The later emergence of the Peyote Cult, which involved not only the exchange of customs and ideas among Indian tribes and the incorporation of Christian concepts, but also intertribal participation in the same ceremonies, carried the process much further and continues to be one of the focal points in Pan-Indianism.

Conspicuous more recent developments are the various powwows and intertribal ceremonial gatherings. Some are organized by the Indians themselves, especially in Oklahoma and the Middle West; others, like the annual Gallup Inter-Tribal Indian Ceremonial, are managed by white businessmen to promote local business interests. But in both types, there is enthusiastic intertribal participation on the part of the Indians and a strong encouragement of Pan-Indianism.

Although the cultural elements found in this emerging Pan-Indian movement are derived from diverse Indian sources, it is highly significant that a high proportion of these elements are drawn from Plains culture: the war bonnet, the Plains-type war dance, and so forth. These elements have become symbols of Indianism to the Indians themselves to a degree that bears little relationship to the aboriginal facts. And it is probable that their importance as symbols derives in part from the fact that these elements are central features of the prevailing white-American stereotype of the American Indian. They are the features of Indian culture which white tourists expect to find when they attend intertribal ceremonials, and Indians are rewarded by the whites for behaving in conformity to the stereotype. This phenomenon is evident at the Gallup Inter-Tribal Ceremonial where a close-to-aboriginal Navaho or Apache dance receives only a scattering of applause, but a Plains-type war dance enjoys a thundering ovation from the white audience, regardless of whether the dance is performed by the Kiowas or by the Zunis! The result is that more and more tribes are adopting Plains styles of dancing, and Pan-Indianism proceeds apace.

Other features of Pan-Indianism include intertribal visiting and intermarriage, which are also of crucial importance, and the national Indian organizations such as the National Congress of American Indians which, to date, are less important than the powwows.

The significance of this Pan-Indianism in general terms is that it provides a social and cultural framework within which acculturating Indian groups can maintain their sense of identity and integrity as Indians as long as the dominant larger society assigns them to subordinate status. In the future, it is probable that this Pan-Indianism will develop greater political significance than it has at present, and that organizations like the National Congress of American Indians will speak more effectively for a more highly organized American-Indian minority which will begin to take the franchise more seriously and be more carefully listened to in the halls of the United States Congress in Washington.

EDWARD H. SPICER (b. 1906) is professor of
anthropology at the University of Arizona and well
known for his book *Cycles of Conquest: The Impact
of Spain, Mexico, and the United States on the
Indians of the Southwest, 1533–1960* (1962) and
numerous other writings. In *A Short History of the
Indians of the United States* (1969) he writes of the
Indians, not from the traditional standpoint of
Indian-white relations, but with a concern for the
continuing development of the Indian communities
themselves. In the final chapter, from which the
following selections are taken, he treats of the
Indians in recent decades. How does the pan-Indianism
he describes consititute a new departure from
traditional Indian community patterns?*

Edward H. Spicer

American Citizens

Chief Justice John Marshall's decision in 1832 did not settle to the satisfaction of all Americans the legal status of Indians. A century later the issues with which Marshall had dealt were still live ones. To some extent they reflected broader questions with which the whole population was concerned, such as the relations between Negroes and Whites, between Jews and Christians, and between European and Oriental immigrants. The terms in which Americans thought about such ethnic relations were sometimes invoked in seeking solutions for "the Indian problem." However, the situation of the Indians, as neither voluntary nor involuntary migrants to the United States, but rather as conquered people with whom treaties had been made until 1871 and whom the Su-preme Court had ruled to be domestic nations, was sharply distinct. Moreover the behavior of Indians in their centuries of resistance to White domination had caught the imagination of Americans and inspired sentiments which led to the Indians' occupying a wholly unique place in American literature and public conscience. The national Congress by the middle of the 20th century had demonstrated that it was inclined to shift its position periodically on the issues which lay at the roots of Indian-White relations, thereby revealing the continuing uncertainty and ambivalence of Americans generally.

Indeed by the 1960s it was clear that a fairly regular cycle of action and reaction had begun to characterize congressional

*From *A Short History of the Indians of the United States,* by Edward H. Spicer. Copyright © 1969 by
Edward H. Spicer, by permission of Van Nostrand Reinhold Company. Pp. 123–127, 139–140, 142–146.

behavior. The underlying issues were not often clearly defined, but there appeared to be two basic ones. The first, around which public discussion and feeling often centered, was the question of whether or not there ought to be any special kind of relationship between the federal government and the Indians, different from any maintained with other residents of the United States. This issue was not to be ignored, for in fact there had been special relationships from the beginning of the republic. A special relationship was a fact of life in the United States, and yet the increasingly dominant value orientation with respect to racial and cultural minorities was that there should be no differences, whether of rights to participate in all citizenship privileges or of freedom from interference by federal agencies in local government. There was, in short, as it appeared to many, a continuing inconsistency in the relationship between government and Indians and the trend in American life toward sanctions against all forms of discrimination among ethnic groups.

The other issue was whether or not Indians should conform to the cultural norms of Anglo-Americans. This, however, was a delicate issue concerning which public discussion was often confused, for the dominant value orientation held that everyone in the United States had a right to choose his own way of life. Therefore many Whites were not inclined to take public positions advocating Anglo conformity, and yet as members of the dominant society whose experience was bounded by the Anglo norms they regarded cultural assimilation to those norms as "inevitable." Few were well enough acquainted with the facts to know that there was no accelerating trend among Indians toward loss of distinctive identity. Thus there existed an inconsistency which was

internal in the dominant White world view, not external as in the case of the special federal relationship. Whites tended to believe at one and the same time in the necessity of Anglo conformity and the desirability of freedom of cultural choice. The ambivalence of Whites was such that the Anglo conformity position was not explicitly expressed in Congressional legislation after 1887–98. Nevertheless sentiments focused around this issue, pro and con, influenced the positions taken in Congress on Indian legislation and were especially influential on the administrative policies of the Bureau of Indian Affairs.

During the century from the 1860s to the 1960s there were two peaks in Congressional action based on dominance of the view that the special governmental relationship should be severed. There were also two peaks based on the opposing view that it should continue. Reaction against the effects of the General Allotment Act led to the first important legislation favoring and defining the continuing special federal relationships. This counter trend to the Dawes Act became clear in 1910, continued through 1924, and reached a culmination in 1934. In 1910 the Congress recognized the chaos in Indian affairs which had been brought about by allotment. The result was a spelling out of new federal trust responsibilities with respect to individual Indian property and definition of trust responsibility for tribal lands. In 1924 the Congress passed an act which granted full citizenship to Indians. This was especially significant because the act was an explicit rejection of the principle underlying the General Allotment Act, namely, that citizenship for Indians should be contingent on individual ownership of land; being born in the United States was now sufficient and conformity to Anglo custom was, implicitly, irrelevant. The process of reversal of national Indian policy culminated in the Indian Reorganization Act of 1934. This not only prohibited further individual allotment and provided for acquisition of more tribal land, but also affirmed the right of Indians to local self-government based on, if Indians so desired, Indian customary law. This was a position consistent with John Marshall's decisions of 1831–32. It involved recognition of the destructive effects on Indian community life of the superintendency and sought to correct the blind spot in federal policy with reference to Indian political existence. Specifically the Indian Reorganization Act provided for voluntary adoption of a tribal council system of representative, constitutional government and for the organization of tribes as business corporations to manage the development of Indian-owned resources.

Within a decade a reaction set in against the newly defined relationship between Indian communities and the nation. The administration of Commissioner of Indian Affairs John Collier was accused of "re-Indianizing the Indians," despite the fact that the tribal council and corporate forms of organization introduced on reservations were basically of the Anglo-American type and not at all like the loose confederacies which had characterized Indian political organization. Slogans such as "Set the Indian Free" began to be heard in Congress and in popular writing. The Bureau of Indian Affairs in 1949 formulated a plan for progressive severing of relations between the Bureau and the tribes in accordance with an "index of acculturation" prepared by the Bureau as a measure of readiness. By 1954, 20 years after the IRA, this approach to Indian affairs had become dominant again among officials of the federal government. It was essentially that of the Dawes Act era, emphasizing again the withdrawal of the federal government. The major difference now was that some effort was being made to secure real information about the condition of the various tribes. It was this increased respect for information which led to the proposal that withdrawal be phased rather than immediately applied to all tribes alike. The legislation embodying the dominance of this approach consisted chiefly in House Concurrent Resolution 108, passed in 1954, which provided for the assumption of responsibility for law and order on reservations by the several states and for "termination" of federal relations with tribes which should vote for termination. The Bureau of Indian Affairs, taking the Congressional mandate, proceeded to apply pressures to two tribes which had long been involved in profitable lumber industries—the Menominee of Wisconsin and the Klamath of Oregon. As termination was carried through for these tribes, an immediate reaction set in against the new-old policy.

Indians, with some individual exceptions, wherever they lived opposed the policy. They were backed by Whites in various national organizations and especially by those who lived in the vicinity of the terminated tribes, who faced new economic and political complexities. The result was a steady swing of the pendulum in the direction of de-emphasizing the termination of the federal relationship. At the same time support grew for taking some of the services to Indians out of the hands of the Bureau of Indian Affairs. In 1956 the United States Public Health Service took over health and medical services. By the late 1960s the trend was towards increasing involvement of various federal agencies in Indian affairs. The agencies newly involved, such as the USPHS and the Office of Economic Opportunity, adopted an approach which emphasized participation of Indian local communities in their programs. The pendulum was swinging, but by 1968 there was no new legislation specific to Indians clearly defining the trend. In 1967, however, a so-called Indian Omnibus Bill was proposed. The bill was submitted first to all tribal councils for discussion and emendation, a development which in itself indicated the nature of the trend towards recognizing the existence of Indian communities as political entities.

The years following the granting of citizenship in 1924 were marked not only by a shifting of the governmental framework regarding Indian affiars, but also by the assumption of active new roles on the part of Indians in national, as well as local, political life. Most notable was the formation of an all-Indian national association in 1944, called the National Congress of American Indians. It represented the emergence of a leadership among Indians which was no longer content to permit organizations founded by Whites, such as the Association on American Indian Affairs and the Indian Rights Association to stand as spokesmen for Indians. This trend continued vigorously through the 1960s, resulting in a variety of organizations and national conferences representing Indian interests in which Indians from various tribes in the United States assumed active leadership. . . .

Terminated Tribes Indian self-sufficiency within American society had been proclaimed as the objective of the General Allotment Act. It was also held to be the aim of the Indian Reorganization Act of 1934. Yet this goal, certainly generally agreed on by the formulators of federal Indian policy, seemed to be elusive. Neither the Dawes Act nor the IRA had, by the 1950s, brought about the generally desired condition. There seemed to be two

horns of the dilemma. On the one hand, there was apparent need for special assistance to Indians in learning the ways of White society. This seemed to call for basic schooling, for experience in the American type of political action, for understanding something of the legal system in which Indian affairs were enmeshed, and for the development of ability in management of individual and tribal resources. The IRA sought to meet these needs in a manner in sharp contrast with the forcing technique adopted in the 1880s. It assumed that the federal government could play an important part in providing this kind of technical assistance and rested on the ground that special relationships between Indians and the government were a necessity of the situation. On the other hand, there was the second horn of the dilemma. The continued helping hand of the federal government led quite obviously to the growth of dependence on the part of Indians on the special institutional framework developed by the Bureau of Indian Affairs. The heart of the dilemma, from the White point of view, was the question how self-sufficiency of Indian societies could develop without governmental assistance and at the same time how it could develop in the constant presence of a governmental bureau.

Federal Withdrawal In the late 1940s, after the resignation of Commissioner John Collier, attention began to focus again in Congress and in the Bureau of Indian Affairs on eliminating the special federal relationship. In 1946 the Congress created the Indian Claims Commission which was designed to provide a means for eliminating once and for all the claims of Indians against the United States for losses of land. If carried through, it was held, this would finally fulfill a basic obligation of the government to Indians. In 1949 a commission under the chairmanship of ex-President Hoover completed investigations into the situation of the Indians and recommended in favor of terminating special administrative relationships. By 1953 the view had become dominant in Congress that the second horn of the dilemma, namely, the severance of government supervision in Indian affairs must take priority in Congressional considerations.

The result was the affirmation of a policy of withdrawal by the federal government. This was expressed in House Concurrent Resolution No. 108 which stated that Indians should be made subject to the same laws as other citizens of the United States as rapidly as possible. It also declared that nine specifically designated groups of Indians and their individual members should be "freed" at the earliest possible time from federal supervision and control and called on the Secretary of the Interior to submit recommendations for bringing this about. The same Congress in 1953 passed Public Law 280 which authorized states to assume responsibility for law and order in Indian areas. In none of the Congressional Acts was mention made of any need for securing Indian consent. The mood of Congress was like that in the 1890s which led to the dissolution of the governments of the Five Civilized Tribes. In effect what was being authorized was a policy directly opposed to that which had guided the legislation of the Indian Reorganization Act.

These Acts of Congress led to further legislation specifically providing for the termination of federal relationship with the nine tribes mentioned in House Concurrent Resolution No. 108. Public Law 587, providing for the termination of the federal trusteeship over the Klamath tribe in Oregon, was passed in 1954, as were similar laws applying to the Alabama-Coushatta of Texas, the Menominee of Wisconsin, and the California Indians. The transfer of federal responsibilities to the state of Texas for the 394 Alabama-Coushatta was desired by the Indians and was quickly accomplished. In the other cases it was not so simple, but the termination action was carried through over a period of three or more years. . . .

Indian Nationalism While federal Indian programs were major determinants in the lives of considerably more than half the Indians of the United States in the period following the granting of citizenship, it was not true that Indian life consisted merely of reactions to the actions of the government. In the midst of the most repressive period of governmental interference, there were new cultural syntheses such as the Native American Church. The federal government did not control Indians, however much it might interfere or help in community development. Indians working along their own lines during the period of the shift to the IRA policy and after came increasingly to influence life in the United States, their own and that of others in a number of different ways. There were indeed two levels of influence. One was regional and the influence here was chiefly on the arts and the daily life of Americans. The other operated at the national level, chiefly on the political and ethical life of the country. Both kinds of influence were a result of the collective impact of Indians as Indians rather than as members of particular tribes, although the influences of particular tribes such as the Navajo and the eastern Cherokee were not absent.

As we have seen, Indians from the very beginning of contact with Whites were stimulated to form confederacies, to unite and confront the Europeans collectively.

We have seen that the movement of the Five Civilized Tribes to Oklahoma led to efforts to form confederacies as a basis for resistance to White pressures that were felt to be coming. At first such movements, like Tecumseh's, were often militant resistance movements to oppose further White encroachment. Later in Indian Territory they were resistance movements also but they no longer looked to military means. Tendencies toward Indian unification of this sort were seriously interfered with by the direct attack of the United States on Indian political life in the 1890s. They were in fact effectively stopped for a time. But at least one concerted resistance movement took form during the 1920s when the land of the Pueblos of New Mexico was suddenly in jeopardy during the corrupt Harding administration. The All Pueblo Council was formed and not only succeeded in getting sufficient national support to stop the efforts to get the Pueblo lands, but also through Anna Wilmarth Ickes, Mary Austin, John Collier, and others who came to know the Pueblos, exerted some intellectual and moral influence on the United States as a whole. Thus by the 1920s the Pueblos were influencing as well as being influenced by general American life.

National Congress of American Indians On a broader scale this kind of impact began to be exerted much more systematically after the 1930s. The influence of John Collier, who did not forget his Pueblo experience, was important in this new development, for as Commissioner of Indian Affairs he encouraged it. In 1944 Indians from various parts of the United States, but at first chiefly from Oklahoma and the Plains, organized a national association called the National Congress of American Indians. It was the first such non-religious, national politi-

cal organization of Indians. Organized as an exclusively Indian membership association, it was in part a reaction against the various White associations which had assumed for themselves the role of spokesmen for Indians. The first president of the NCAI was Judge N. B. Johnson, a "mixed blood" Cherokee from eastern Oklahoma who served for eight terms. Later presidents and important officers came from among Plains tribes, Pueblos, Western Apaches, and others. The NCAI had a number of aims, but chief among them were keeping an eye on legislation before the Congress and disseminating more realistic information about Indians. The first of these led to a lobbying organization in Washington which effectively worked against legislation harmful to Indian interests, as conceived by the NCAI, and for favorable legislation. The second objective led to the publication of a regular periodical which not only served to provide more accurate information but also became a forum for Indians all over the country and thus became a means of increasing Indian interaction and solidarity. The NCAI continued as an active organization and became increasingly influential as spokesman for an important segment at least of the Indian population. Its influence was considerable through an especially able succession of executive directors, such as Ruth Muskrat Bronson, Helen Peterson, and Vine Deloria. By the 1960s, it had become an important political influence nationally on Indian affairs.

By the same time there had begun to grow, inevitably, some dissatisfaction with the NCAI. Younger Indians sometimes held that it was dominated by "mixed bloods" and felt that other viewpoints needed expression. In 1961 a National Indian Youth Council was organized in which younger Indians began to exert influence at the national level in the manner of the NCAI. The NIYC was influenced by the rising tide of popular movements of the times and in 1964 became active in a demonstration in the northwest known as a "fish-in" which sought to remind the country that Indians had prior rights in important fishing streams. It also published a journal and made an effort to pay special attention to educational problems of Indian youth. These two organizations were indicative of the increasingly effective participation of Indians in national politics and public education. They were supra-tribal. They expressed a solidarity which had been forced on Indians by the long period of identical pressures applied to all Indians alike. Tribal differences were merged in the national interest of Indians under pressure. Both organizations by the 1960s were vigorous in their affirmation of certain values which they defined as Indian and in which they expressed pride. They constantly attacked the belief that Anglo conformity was inevitable. They adopted a program of needling the complacency of the dominant society about Anglo-American cultural values which they rated as inferior to Indian values.

Pan-Indianism These two organizations were major expressions of what may be called a nationalistic movement among Indians. Indians had developed a common consciousness an an ethnic group, in part goaded by actions of the United States government. They were actively at work to combat those actions and to gain practical advantages through the usual political means in the United States, but also to affirm and make clear to the rest of the country the Indians' right to choose their own ways of life. Below the level of such national action

and affirmation, there were more localized movements of particular tribal groups. For action at the national level did not mean that there had taken place any general mergence of separate tribal identities. On the contrary, everywhere in the United States there were strong resurgences or continuities in tribal consciousness. Among the eastern Cherokees under their tribal council system an historical pageant "Unto These Hills" was instituted which became a major summer festival for many thousands of Indians and non-Indians. The pageant was merely one of many indicators of the growth of tribal pride in what had been for many years a submerged people in North Carolina. In New York State there was similar growth during the 1950s of a nationalistic spirit among the Senecas. Navajo, Sioux, Hopi, Fox, Ute, and many others were moving along the same path. They were asserting themselves in various ways, stimulated by the changing national conception of Indians assisted by the national organizations and also by the post-1934 approach of the Bureau of Indian Affairs and other government agencies.

These political expressions of Indian life rested in part on cultural developments of many years standing, on what had been labelled Pan-Indianism. This term had been applied to the sharing of common interests by Indians of many tribes in certain dances, ceremonials, and music of the Plains and Oklahoma tribes. In different parts of the country, most notably in Oklahoma where many different tribes had been thrown together, but also in the northern plains and the Great Lakes area, annual "powwows" and similar gatherings brought together Indians of various tribal origins. During the 1940s and 1950s the scope of such gatherings widened and they increased greatly in numbers. They stimulated interchange of costumes, dances, songs, and ceremonial paraphernalia. By the 1960s the whole of the United States was linked by a system of annual summer powwows or "ceremonials." The common experience of Indians as reservation dwellers and as persons of Indian cultural heritage was pooled. To some extent the situation was contributed to by the fact that the boarding schools had also brought Indians of different tribes together, often with resulting intertribal marriages. There was thus a growing common pool of selected Indian cultural elements and interests. "Pan-Indianism" was undoubtedly one important basis for the Indian political consciousness which expressed itself in the national organizations.

A Sioux Indian, VINE DELORIA, JR. (b. 1934) was
director of the National Congress of American Indians
from 1964 to 1967. His book *Custer Died for Your
Sins: An Indian Manifesto* (1969) is a hard-hitting,
sometimes intemperate, often witty indictment of
American treatment of the Indians by anthropologists,
missionaries, and government officials and a plea that
Indians be allowed to direct their own destinies.
Although Deloria does not claim to speak for all
Indians, his writings have forced many white Americans
to reconsider their attitudes toward their red brothers.
The article printed here exhibits the attributes of
Indians who are ready to speak out forcefully in
support of their rights.*

Vine Deloria, Jr.

The War Between the Redskins
and the Feds

If Secretary of the Interior Walter
Hickel has any sense of history, he must
have been impressed with his situation at
the convention of the National Congress
of American Indians held earlier this fall
in Alburqueque, N.M. Not since George
Armstrong Custer's sensitivity-training
session on the banks of the Little Big
Horn had so many angry Indians surrounded a representative of the United
States Government with blood in their
eyes. Of the estimated million Indians
in the United States, the N.C.A.I. repre-
sents the reservation population of some
400,000. With spokesmen for the remaining urban and other Indian communities
of the East (500,000 urban Indians and
100,000 scattered Eastern bands) attending
the convention, Hickel was greeted by

representatives of the entire Indian community, including Eskimos, Indians and
Aleuts from his home state of Alaska.

All summer, tension had been building
within the Indian community as the
tribes fearfully awaited the pronouncement of Indian policy by the new Nixon
Administration. During the 1968 Presidential campaign Nixon had promised
that, if elected, he would not unilaterally
sever Federal relations with the tribes,
nor would he allow the tribes to be pres-
sured to alter the relationship themselves.
Indian leadership, recalling that Nixon
had been Vice President during the Eisen-
hower Administration, when the hated
policy of termination of Federal responsibilities for Indians had been forced on
the unwary tribes, was alerted for any

signs of change, and skeptical of the "New Federalism."

Hickel's performance in 1969 appeared to have justified Indian suspicions. In late July, at a Western Governors' Conference in Seattle, he characterized the relationship of the Federal Government as "overprotective" of Indian rights. With a foot-in-mouth aplomb so characteristic of some of Nixon's interchangeable Cabinet members, Hickel compounded this error by labeling the reservations as "crutches" by which Indians avoided their full responsibilities as citizens.

By late summer, the moccasin telegraph was buzzing with rumors that the new Secretary of the Interior was a "terminationist," and that a great battle over the very existence of the reservations was imminent. Indian reservations have a total land base of more than 52 billion acres, scattered in 26 states and providing a home for people of 315 different tribal groups. The life expectancy of a reservation Indian is 46 years, rising nearly a year each year under current programs. Although the average income is slightly over $1,500 per family annually, and the housing is generally substandard, the reservations are all that remain of the continent the Indians once owned, and they are determined to fight for every handful of dust that remains.

The National Traditionalist Movement, spearheaded by the Iroquois League, called for Hickel's removal from office. The Iroquois (the only Indian tribe to declare war on Germany in 1917) set a strong nationalistic tone to the resistance, which quickly sprang up in Indian country.

From the urban Indian centers on the West Coast, the third-world-oriented United Native Americans took up the battle cry. "IMPEACH HICKEL" bumper stickers blossomed beside "Red Power"

and the multitude of "Custer" slogans on Indian cars. Petitions calling for Hickel's removal began to circulate on the Coast.

As the N.C.A.I. convention opened, there was considerable discussion by the delegates as to the length at which Indians should *stabilize* Hickel's hairline. This remark was an obvious reference to Hickel's conception of his role as trustee in defending the water rights of the Pyramid Lake Paiutes of Nevada. The Pyramid Lake tribe has a beautiful lake, the largest fresh-water lake in the state. For the major part of this century it has tried to insure that sufficient water is delivered to the lake to maintain its excellent cutthroat trout fishery and its flock of pelicans. But the Federal Government has continually refused to defend the tribe's water rights by allowing other users to take water which is rightfully owned by the Paiutes. Consequently, the lake has had a declining shoreline for most of the century, a condition that precludes development of the reservation for recreation purposes.

Hickel's solution, proposed after a meeting with Governors Reagan of California and Laxalt of Nevada, was to reduce the water level 152 feet, creating a mud flat of 40,000 acres and thus "stabilizing" the water level. It was the same logic used by the Army to destroy a Vietnamese village—"We had to destroy the village to save it." It naturally followed that the only way to save Pyramid Lake was to drain it.

With these remarks to his credit, it is a wonder that Hickel was the recipient of only sporadic boos and catcalls when he attempted to address the Indian convention. No one even speculated on the possibility of a canine ancestor in Hickel's immediate family tree. "Terminationist" is a much dirtier word in the Indian vocabulary.

Wally Hickel is not that bad a guy. He was genuinely puzzled by the reactions which his remarks had created in the Indian community. In his own mind he was simply searching for a new approach to a problem that he, as Secretary of the Interior, had a responsibility to resolve. But he had unexpectedly hit the one nerve which had been frayed raw by a century of abuse and betrayal: the treaty-trust relationship between Indians and the Federal Government.

Hickel's remarks at Seattle and on the water problems in Nevada prior to the meeting of the National Congress of American Indians fitted exactly into prior speeches and problems of other times and places which had resulted in policies and programs destructive of the reservation communities. He could not have said anything more inflammatory than that the Federal Government had been "over-protective" of Indian rights, implying that the Government would be less zealous in fulfilling its responsibilities during his tenure as Secretary of the Interior. . . .

Until 1871 the tribes were treated as sovereign yet dependent domestic nations with whom the Federal Government was bound to treat for land cessions. In the treaties, the Government accepted the responsibility to protect the lands reserved by the tribes for their own use against encroachments by its own citizens. In that year, however, Congress decided that it would sign no more treaties with tribes. Instead, a policy emerged aimed at breaking up the tribal structures, even though the United States had promised in good faith that it would not interfere with traditional tribal customs and laws.

The shift in policy placed major emphasis on enticing, threatening, or deceiving individual Indians into forsaking their tribal relations. A comparable situation would exist if the Government re-fused to recognize General Motors as a corporation and insisted that it would become concerned with the individual stockholders, enticing them to sell their stock and liquidating the assets of the corporation, all the while wondering why General Motors was declining as an economic entity.

The tribes fought back. Asserting that the treaties were contracts between two parties, the tribe and the Federal Government, they often punished with death any leaders who signed away tribal rights. While fundamental logic supported the tribal position, overwhelming power and deceit by Government officials were able to carry the day. The treaties had been signed by nations, not an arbitrary conglomerate of individuals. Yet the official Federal policy was to assimilate the individual Indians even if their rights as members of tribes had to be breached.

A major influence against the tribes was the ideology of the missionaries who were attempting to force their own ideas of culture on the captive audiences on the reservations. The missionaries believed that only by inculcating selfishness and the concept of private property into tribal society would individual Indians be able to become Christians and be saved.

Church pressure to individualize the tribes and dispose of the tribal land estate resulted in the passage of the Dawes Act in 1887. This act divided the reservations up into allotments of 160 acres, and each Indian was given a piece of land for farming. The remainder of the tribal holdings was declared "surplus" and opened to settlement by non-Indians.

Before allotment was forced on the tribes, there was no poverty on the reservations. The minority report issued against the policy mentioned the complete absence of pauperism among the Five Civilized Tribes of Oklahoma. It suggested that the Indian method of holding land for an entire community might be superior to the idea of non-Indian society, in that this method precluded a class of people that was perennially poor, while non-Indian society was plagued with poverty in its lower economic class.

The effect of individualizing the tribal estate was the creation of extreme poverty on many of the reservations. Individual Indians, unaccustomed to viewing land as a commodity, were easily swindled out of their allotments. Good farm land often went for a bottle of liquor, white trustees of individual Indian estates often mysteriously inherited their wards' property, and dying Indians were known to have mysteriously given their lands to churches before expiring. One Indian commissioner trod on eggshells during his term because a half-million-dollar Indian estate passed on to a missionary society instead of to the Indian heirs. Between 1887 and 1934 some 90 million acres of land left Indian ownership in a variety of ways. The actual circumstances in some cases have never seen the light of day.

Indians who sold their lands did not merge into white society and disappear. They simply moved onto their relatives' lands and remained within the tribal society. Thus, the land base was rapidly diminishing while the population continued to remain constant and, in some cases, grew spectacularly.

The situation had become so bad by 1926 that a massive study was authorized. It was called the Meriam Survey, and it pointed out that if the allotment process was not solved, the United States would soon have on its hands a landless, pauperized Indian population totally incapable of succeeding in American society.

In 1933, the New Deal Administration appointed John Collier as Indian Affairs Commissioner. He helped to write into law the basic charter of Indian rights called the Indian Reorganization Act. Indian tribes were given status as Federal corporations under this act, allotment was stopped and efforts were made to rebuild a land base for the Indian communities.

Tribal governments allocated a substantial portion of tribal income to purchase the allotments of individual Indians, thus holding in Indian hands the land that would have been lost forever. Tribes began their gradual revival of traditional ways, and were making excellent progress when World War II caused a dreadful reduction in domestic spending. Programs could not be funded until after the war.

In 1954 the chairmanship of the Indian Subcommittee of the Senate Interior Committee was taken over by Senator Arthur Watkins of Utah. Watkins was an archconservative who understood nothing of Indian treaties, was contemptuous of Indian people, and was determined to solve the "Indian problem" in his short tenure as chairman of the committee. He began a unilateral war against Indian communities that was known as "termination."

Watkins visualized himself as the Abraham Lincoln of the 20th century. Characterizing the reservations as havens of irresponsibility, and accepting the thesis that the Federal Government had been too protective of Indian rights, the Senator was determined to break the long-standing commitments of the United States to its Indian tribes—whether it was just or not.

"With the aim of 'equality before the law' in mind, our course should rightly be no other," Watkins announced. "Firm and constant consideration for those of Indian ancestry should lead us all to work diligently with all other Americans. Following in the footsteps of the Emancipation Proclamation of 94 years ago, I see the following words emblazoned in letters of fire above the heads of the Indians—THESE PEOPLE SHALL BE FREE."

If Watkins was determined to *free* the Indians, he was a generation too late. In 1924 the Indian Citizens Act was passed making all noncitizen Indians American citizens with full rights and privileges. The act further declared that the "granting of such citizenship shall not in any manner impair or otherwise affect the right of any Indians to tribal or other property."

The Indian Citizens Act thus gave full constitutional rights to individual Indians insofar as they were individuals. It specifically exempted any rights that individual Indians may have had in tribal property from its operation. The dual citizenship of Indian people was thus recognized.

But Watkins was convinced that holding an interest in tribal property in addition to holding citizenship was a handicap. Under this theory, everyone who benefited from a trust fund was automatically a second-class citizen.

A number of tribes fell victim to Watkins's crusade. The Menominees owned a forest in Wisconsin. They had a tribal sawmill and operated it to provide employment for tribal members, rather than to make a profit—although with their exemption from corporate taxation they often showed a profit. The tribe spent most of its income on social services, supporting its own hospital and providing its own law enforcement on the reservation. It was more genuinely a self-supporting community than many non-Indian communities near it.

Termination of Federal supervision meant an immediate tax bill of 55 per cent on the sawmill. To meet this, the saw mill had to be automated, thus throwing a substantial number of Indians out of work and onto the unemployment rolls. To meet the rising unemployment situation, the only industry, the sawmill, had to be taxed by the county. There was an immediate spiral downward in the capital structure of the tribe so that, in the years since the termination bill was passed, it had to receive some $10-million in special state and Federal aid. The end is not yet in sight.

When the smoke had cleared, some 8,000 Indians had been deprived of rights their grandfathers had dearly purchased through land cessions. The Paiutes of Utah and Klamaths of Oregon were caught in a private trusteeship more restrictive than their original Federal trust relationship, from which they were to have been "freed." Fortunately, Texas made a tourist attraction out of the Alabama-Coushatta reservation in that state, thus preserving most of the tribal assets. The mixed-blood Utes of Utah formed their own organization and tried to remain together as a community. The Siletz and Grande Ronde Indians of Oregon, the California Indians, and the Catawbas of South Carolina simply vanished. Menominee County became the most depressed county in the nation.

In Watkins's mind, and in the mind of his successors on the Senate Interior Committee, the opportunity to remake American Indians into small businessmen was too much of a temptation. The termination policy continued to roll in spite of its catastrophic effects on the Indian communities.

Tribes refused to consider any programs, feeling that it was no use to build good houses when the reservation might be sold out from under them at any time. Development schemes to upgrade reservation resources were turned down by people with no apparent future. The progress which had been made by the tribes under the Indian Reorganization Act ground to a halt. Indian people spent a decade in limbo, hesitant to make any plans for fear they would come under attack by the irrational policy.

Watkins's rationale at the beginning had been that he was making the individual Indians first-class citizens, where they previously had been handicapped by maintaining their tribal relationships. It was the same reasoning that had led policymakers in the last century to force allotment on the tribes and create the original poverty conditions on the reservations. When the termination legislation was finally drawn for the Menominees, the concluding phrase in section 10 of the bill was illuminating: "Nothing in this act shall affect the status of the members of the tribe as citizens of the United States"!

The argument of "freeing" the Indians was as phony as could be. The act did nothing but dissipate tribal capital and destroy the rights of Indian tribes to have their own communities. But termination fitted exactly into the integrationist-thought world of the period, and the expanding Civil Rights movement of the black community, which had been given impetus by the decision of *Brown v. Topeka Board of Education,* the famous school desegration case of 1954. So it *seemed* the right thing to do.

Society has come a long way in its understanding of itself since 1954. The ensuing civil rights movement, which had shaken the foundations of society during the nineteen-fifties, changed abruptly into the black power movements of the late sixties. For half a decade we have been struggling to define the place of a group of people in American society and, as numerous reports have indicated, the divisions in the society have become more

pronounced, the hatreds more violent and lasting.

Termination slowed down during the Kennedy-Johnson Administrations, but the basic Congressional directive has never been changed. Policy-makers in Congress and in the Interior Department continue to regard decisions made in haste in 1954 as imperatives which they must follow today. Only by a vigilant National Congress of American Indians watching the Washington scene day and night have Indian people been able to stop further implementation of this policy.

Walter Hickel, in his casual remarks, stirred up a hornet's nest of Indian concern. It did not seem possible to tribal leaders that the new Administration would return to a policy proven bankrupt when it was applied to their land holdings in 1887, again proven bankrupt in 1954 with the further dissipation of their remaining lands and resources, and completely out of tune with the social movements of today.

Indian tribes have been able, in spite of all pressures exerted against them, and the failure of the Federal Government to defend their rights, to maintain a capital in land and resources by which they can maintain their own communities. They have been able to keep tribal governments alive and functioning. In the War on Poverty, tribes provided services for all people within reservation boundaries, red or white, and many children received services that they would not have otherwise received because their counties did not want to sponsor programs under the Office of Economic Opportunity.

The record of Indian people as a recognized self-governing community is enlightening. The progress of the last decade is spectacular and sophisticated for a people with a national average of eight years of education. Indian people are now demanding control of education programs through the creation of Indian reservation school boards. They are certain they can do better than either the state or Federal education they have been given in the past. The variety of projects undertaken by Indian communities is staggering and encompasses everything from sawmills to ocean-going fishing vessels, motels to carpet factories.

American society has much to learn from Indian tribes. It may all be lost if another era of struggle over reservation existence is initiated. The black community, spearheaded by the demands for reparations by James Forman, is desperately seeking capital funds. Indian tribes already have capital in land and resources and have demonstrated how well it can be used.

Blacks and Mexicans are developing rural cooperatives in an effort to solve the poverty of their people in the rural areas. Indian tribes have already proven that rural corporations and cooperatives can and do work when undertaken by a united community.

Conservationists are pointing out the rapidly dwindling natural resources of the nation, the danger of total extinction of life unless strong conservation practices are begun at once. The Quinault and Lummi Indian tribes have already zoned their beaches to conserve their natural state, while the White Mountain Apaches have developed nearly 30 artifical lakes and maintain the best fishing and recreation areas in Arizona.

The power movements, the Amish situation in the Midwest, the desire of the Acadians in Louisiana to have French taught in schools, the conflict between the ethnic groups in the urban areas, all point toward new social concepts revolving around a number of ethnic and racial communities desiring to conduct their own affairs. Even the rising conservative trend in politics seeks power at the local level rather than continued direction from long distance.

Tribes have overcome enmities of the past. They were once far deeper and more bitter than in the current impasse between black and white. Unemployment is declining as tribal programs are committed to creating jobs, not simply making profits. Land is being renewed, beaches and rivers are being cleared and the reservations are becoming models of proper land use. Indian society is stabilizing itself to face the instantaneous electric world of today far better than are other segments of American society.

The Indian outrage at Hickel was a cry to society at large. "If you destroy us," it really said, "you will destroy your last chance to understand who you are, where you have been, and where you have to go next in order to survive as a people." One hopes Secretary Hickel and the Senators and Congressmen will hear this cry and understand.

Suggested Readings

An excellent brief survey of the history of Indian-white relations in the United States is William T. Hagan, *American Indians* (Chicago, 1961). The same author has prepared a useful bibliographical essay, *The Indian in American History* (New York, 1963). A recent general volume, which emphasizes the history of the Oklahoma Indians, is Angie Debo, *A History of the Indians of the United States* (Norman, Okla., 1970). Of value also is *The American Heritage Book of Indians* (New York, 1961), which is notable for its magnificent illustrations. The text of this book, written by William Brandon, has been published separately in paperback (New York, 1964). Another general book which contains useful material is Oliver LaFarge, *A Pictorial History of the American Indian* (New York, 1956). A brief history written by an Indian scholar is D'Arcy McNickle, *They Came Here First: The Epic of the American Indian* (Philadelphia, 1949). Two collections of documents which have been compiled to present a broad picture of Indian-white relations are Wilcomb E. Washburn, ed., *The Indian and the White Man* (Garden City, N.Y., 1964) and Jack D. Forbes, ed., *The Indian in America's Past* (Englewood Cliffs, N.J., 1964). Both of these exhibit a viewpoint critical of white actions. Edward H. Spicer, *A Short History of the Indians of the United States* (New York, 1969) provides an extensive selection of documents in addition to a history of the development of Indian communities.

For the history of early Indian-white relations an excellent guide is the article printed in this book by Bernard W. Sheehan, "Indian-White Relations in Early America: A Review Essay," *William and Mary Quarterly*, 3rd ser., XXVI (April, 1969), 267–286. The text and footnotes of this article furnish extensive references and an able critique. For the colonial period, special note should be made of Wilcomb E. Washburn, "The Moral and Legal Justifications for Dispossessing the Indians," in James Morton Smith, ed., *Seventeenth Century America: Essays in Colonial History* (Chapel Hill, N.C., 1959); Alden T. Vaughan, *New England Frontier: Puritans and Indians, 1620–1675* (Boston, 1965); Douglas E. Leach, *Flintlock and Tomahawk: New England in King Philip's War* (New York, 1958); and Allen W. Trelease, *Indian Affairs in Colonial New York: The Seventeenth Century* (Ithaca, N.Y., 1960). For the southern Indian frontier, see Verner W. Crane, *The Southern Frontier, 1670–1732* (Ann Arbor, Mich., 1929) and John R. Alden, *John Stuart and the Southern Colonial Frontier: A Study of Indian Relations, War, Trade, and Land Problems in the Southern Wilderness, 1754–1775* (Ann Arbor, Mich., 1944).

Indian affairs in the United States in the first half of the nineteenth century can be traced in Reginald Horsman, *Expansion and American Indian Policy, 1783–1812* (East Lansing, Mich., 1967); Francis Paul Prucha, *American Indian Policy in the Formative Years: The Indian Trade and Intercourse Acts, 1790–1834* (Cambridge, Mass., 1962); and an older work by George D. Harmon, *Sixty Years of Indian Affairs: Political, Economic, and Diplomatic, 1789–1850* (Chapel Hill, N.C., 1941). Roy Harvey Pearce, *Savagism and Civilization: A Study of the Indian and the American Mind* (Baltimore, 1967) is a history of the beliefs the white Americans held in the period up to 1851. It was originally published in 1953 under the title, *The Savages of America: The Study of the Indian and the Idea of Civilization.*

More specialized works dealing with the

removal of the eastern Indians to lands west of the Mississippi are Grant Foreman's *Indian Removal: The Emigration of the Five Civilized Tribes of Indians* (new ed., Norman, Okla., 1953) and his *The Last Trek of the Indians* (Chicago, 1946). A highly documented, dispassionate history of official actions leading to removal is Annie H. Abel, "The History of Events Resulting in Indian Consolidation West of the Mississippi," *Annual Report of the American Historical Association for the Year 1906,* I, 233–450. A much more readable account of removal, though less objective, is Dale Van Every, *Disinherited: The Lost Birthright of the American Indian* (New York, 1966). A series of readings on Cherokee removal is provided in Louis Filler and Allen Guttmann, eds., *The Removal of the Cherokee Nation: Manifest Destiny or National Dishonor* (Boston, 1962). The story of Indian allotments in connection with removal is Mary E. Young, *Redskins, Ruffleshirts and Rednecks: Indian Land Allotments in Alabama and Mississippi, 1830–1860* (Norman, Okla., 1961). The widely accepted idea that the eastern Indians were moved to worthless lands in the West is refuted in Francis Paul Prucha, "Indians Removal and the Great American Desert," *Indiana Magazine of History,* LIX (December, 1963), 299–322.

Changes in Indian policy after 1840 are discussed in James C. Malin, *Indian Policy and Westward Expansion* (Lawrence, Kans., 1921), while Indian relations after the Mexican War are analyzed in the monograph by Alban W. Hoopes, *Indian Affairs and Their Administration: With Special Reference to the Far West, 1849–1860* (Philadelphia, 1932). Annie H. Abel, in her three-volume work *The Slaveholding Indians* (Cleveland, 1915–1925) tells the story of the Five Civilized Tribes and their relations with the Confederacy.

Three works deal with the movement for Indian reform and assimilation in the post-Civil War decades. The attempt of the Grant administration to solve the problems of Indian affairs by turning the Indian agencies over to missionary groups is studied in Peter J. Rahill, *The Catholic Indian Missions and Grant's Peace Policy, 1870–1884* (Washington,

1953), which treats specifically of Catholic activities. Henry E. Fritz, on the other hand, in *The Movement for Indian Assimilation, 1860–1890* (Philadelphia, 1963), writes more from a Protestant viewpoint. Loring Benson Priest, *Uncle Sam's Stepchildren: The Reformation of United States Indian Policy, 1865–1887* (New Brunswick, N.J., 1942) is concerned chiefly with the movements leading up to the Dawes Act. The effect of the Dawes Act upon one tribe is told in Angie Debo, *And Still the Waters Run* (Princeton, N.J., 1940), which chronicles the actions of lawyers and land speculators to separate the Choctaws from their land. The working out of the act in a northern tribe is discussed in Roy W. Meyer, *History of the Santee Sioux: United States Indian Policy on Trial* (Lincoln, Nebr., 1967), which treats in detail the operation of federal legislation in both the nineteenth and twentieth centuries.

Opposition to the principles of allotting lands to the Indians in severalty and to the forced erosion of Indian culture led in the 1920s and 1930s to a reversal of the Dawes Act philosophy. The development of this reform is traced in Randolph C. Downes, "A Crusade for Indian Reform, 1922–1934," *Mississippi Valley Historical Review,* XXXII (December, 1945), 331–354. The "New Deal" for the Indians under the Indian Reorganization Act of 1934 and its aftermath are discussed in S. Lyman Tyler, *Indian Affairs: A Study of the Changes in Policy of the United States Toward Indians* (Provo, Utah, 1964) and in John Collier, *Indians of the Americas: The Long Hope* (New York, 1947).

The only available study devoted specifically to the Bureau of Indian Affairs is Laurence F. Schmeckebier, *The Office of Indian Affairs: Its History, Activities and Organization* (Baltimore, 1927), but most books on Indian affairs treat of the Bureau in some detail, often in a critical fashion. Useful information on Indian agents is found in Ruth A. Gallaher, "The Indian Agent in the United States Before 1850," *Iowa Journal of History and Politics,* XIV (January, 1916), 3–55, and Flora W. Seymour, *Indian Agents of the Old Frontier* (New York, 1941). The story of one noted agent is told in Merritt B. Pound, *Benjamin Hawkins, Indian Agent* (Athens, Ga., 1951). A detailed treatment of land tenure problems is J. P. Kinney, *A Continent Lost—A Civilization Won: Indian Land Tenure in America* (Baltimore, 1937); the author presents a favorable view of Indian Bureau activities.

Biographies of Indian leaders furnish insight into Indian character and the relations between the races. A unique autobiography is that of Black Hawk; the best edition is Donald Jackson, ed., *Ma-Ka-Tai-Me-She-Kia-Kiak— Black Hawk: An Autobiography* (Urbana, Ill., 1955). Brief sketches of Indian leaders make up Alvin M. Josephy, Jr., *The Patriot Chiefs: A Chronicle of American Indian Leadership* (New York, 1961). See also Anthony F. C. Wallace, *King of the Delawares: Teedyuscung, 1700–1763* (Philadelphia, 1949); Howard H. Peckham, *Pontiac and the Indian Uprising* (Princeton, N.J., 1947); and Glenn Tucker, *Tecumseh: Vision of Glory* (Indianapolis, 1956).

Missionary activity among the Indians is studied in Robert F. Berkhofer, Jr., *Salvation and the Savage: An Analysis of Protestant Missions and American Indian Response, 1787–1862* (Lexington, Ky., 1965) and in R. Pierce Beaver, *Church, State, and the American Indians: Two and a Half Centuries of Partnership in Missions Between Protestant Churches and Government* (St. Louis, 1966). A more detailed and specialized work is Robert Ignatius Burns, *The Jesuits and the Indian Wars of the Northwest* (New Haven, Conn., 1966). On Indian education, see Evelyn C. Adams, *American Indian Education: Government Schools and Economic Progress* (New York, 1946).

Much of the history of Indian affairs in the United States has been written in terms of individual tribes. An outstanding group of such histories is found in the Civilization of the American Indian Series published by the University of Oklahoma Press. Representative volumes in the series are Angie Debo, *The Rise and Fall of the Choctaw Republic* (1934); George E. Hyde, *Red Cloud's Folk: A History of the Oglala Sioux Indians* (1937); Morris L. Wardell, *A Political History of the Chero-*

kee Nation, 1838–1907 (1938); Ernest Wallace and E. Adamson Hoebel, *The Comanches: Lords of the South Plains* (1952); Ruth M. Underhill, *The Navajos* (1956); William T. Hagan, *The Sac and Fox Indians* (1958); John C. Ewers, *The Blackfeet: Raiders on the Northwestern Plains* (1958); C. L. Sonnichsen, *The Mescalero Apaches* (1958); John Joseph Mathews, *The Osages: Children of the Middle Waters* (1961); and Donald J. Berthrong, *The Southern Cheyennes* (1963). Other valuable works dealing with specific aspects of individual tribes are James C. Olsen, *Red Cloud and the Sioux Problem* (Lincoln, Nebr., 1965); Robert M. Utley, *The Last Days of the Sioux Nation* (New Haven, Conn., 1963), which gives a remarkably balanced account of the Wounded Knee Massacre of 1890; and Lawrence C. Kelly, *The Navajo Indians and Federal Indian Policy* (Tucson, 1968), which covers the period 1900–1935.

The condition of the Indians in mid-twentieth century can be viewed in the following volumes of collected essays: David A. Baerreis, ed., *The Indian in Modern America* (Madison, Wis., 1956); "American Indians and American Life," vol. 311 (May, 1957), *Annals of the American Academy of Political and Social Science;* and Nancy O. Lurie and Stewart Levine, eds., *The American Indian Today* (Deland, Fla., 1968). *The Indian: America's Unfinished Business* (Norman, Okla., 1966) is a report, compiled by William A. Brophy and Sophie D. Aberle, of the Commission on the Rights, Liberties, and Responsibilities of the American Indian. Stan Steiner, *The New Indians* (New York, 1968) is a moving journalistic account of the awakening of political consciousness of present-day Indians. Vine Deloria, Jr., in *Custer Died for Your Sins: An Indian Manifesto* (New York, 1969), forcefully presents an Indian's view of Indian-white relations. *Our Brother's Keeper: The Indian in White America* (New York, 1969), edited by Edgar S. Cohn, is an indictment of the condition and treatment of the Indians today. The opinions and attitudes of Indians can be found in a new Indian-edited journal, *The Indian Historian.*

Students who want to get general anthropological background for their historical study of Indian affairs will find useful Clark Wissler, *Indians of the United States: Four Centuries of Their History and Culture* (New York, 1940) and Ruth M. Underhill, *Red Man's America: A History of Indians in the United States* (Chicago, 1953). A more recent general textbook is Harold E. Driver, *Indians of North America* (Chicago, 1961). Alvin M. Josephy, Jr., *The Indian Heritage of America* (New York, 1968) provides brief surveys of the archeology, ethnology, and history of the various Indian cultures of North America. A fascinating booklet is D'Arcy McNickle, *The Indian Tribes of the United States: Ethnic and Cultural Survival* (London, 1962). For an interesting comparative history, see A. Grenfell Price, *White Settlers and Native Peoples: An Historical Study of Racial Contacts between En-glish-speaking Whites and Aboriginal Peoples in the United States, Canada, Australia and New Zealand* (Melbourne, 1949).

Important reference works on Indians are Frederick W. Hodge, ed., *Handbook of American Indians North of Mexico* (Washington, 1907–1910), an encyclopedic collection of short articles on historical and ethnological topics; Charles J. Kappler, ed., *Indian Laws and Treaties* (Washington, 1904), which prints exact copies of the treaties made between the Indians and the United States; Charles C. Royce, *Indian Land Cessions in the United States* (Washington, 1899), which describes in detail all land cessions made by the Indians and marks them out on a series of state maps; and Felix S. Cohen, *Handbook of Federal Indian Law* (Washington, 1941).